The Plant Closure Policy Dilemma

LABOR, LAW AND BARGAINING

Wayne R. Wendling

1984

The W. E. Upjohn Institute for Employment Research

Library of Congress Cataloging in Publication Data

Wendling, Wayne R.
  The plant closure policy dilemma.

  Bibliography: p.

  1. Plant shutdowns—Government policy—United States.
  2. Plant shutdowns—Law and legislation—United States.
  3. Collective bargaining—United States.   4. Labor laws
  and legislation—United States.   5. Labor policy—United
  States.   I. Title.
  HD5708.55.U6W46   1984   338.6'042   84-10387
  ISBN 0-88099-019-8
  ISBN 0-88099-020-1 (pbk.)

THE INSTITUTE, a nonprofit research organization, was established
on July 1, 1945. It is an activity of the W. E. Upjohn Unemployment
Trustee Corporation, which was formed in 1932 to administer a fund set
aside by the late Dr. W. E. Upjohn for the purpose of carrying on
"research into the causes and effects of unemployment and measures for
the alleviation of unemployment."

ii

ACKNOWLEDGMENTS

The idea for this book emerged in 1981. The economy was entering its second downturn in a year, plant closure legislation was being discussed in many states, and there was a feeling of despair about the future of manufacturing employment in the United States. As I read the articles and books on the plant closure problem that were coming out at that time, I was struck by the virtual exclusion of a very important institution—collective bargaining—as a possible means of resolving or mitigating the problems associated with plant closure. That prompted me to examine the potential of collective bargaining to help resolve the chronic problems associated with plant closure.

No idea becomes a book without the advice and assistance of colleagues, mentors, support staff and family. I would like to express my gratitude to the individuals who were so crucial to the completion of this study. My colleagues at the W. E. Upjohn Institute for Employment Research provided critical review of my thinking and writing. Richard Perlman, my teacher for over a decade, reviewed the entire document and, as has been his trademark, offered far more constructive comments than one is worthy to receive. The late E. Earl Wright, former director of the Institute, encouraged me to explore the plant closure problem. I would also like to express my appreciation to Denise Duquette for her technical support of the numerous drafts of this document.

Finally, my wife, Barbara Monroe, reacted to ideas, edited my drafts and helped to create an environment conducive to this effort. Her contribution has been immeasurable.

FOREWORD

Economic and political hardships associated with plant closure may be easily forgotten in the current environment of real growth, rising capacity utilization and declining unemployment. However, plant closure is an ongoing, chronic problem, which does not disappear during times of economic recovery. We need to consider policy options that recognize the tenacity, special nature, and institutional context of this problem.

Collective bargaining appears to be the institutional context in which the solution to the plant closure problem is most likely to be found. Since labor costs, work rules and productivity frequently are cited as reasons for closure, collective bargaining appears to be the mechanism ideally suited to resolving these issues. However, critics of collective bargaining have emphasized that unions have only one objective: delaying closure as long as possible.

This study contains a new proposal on the use of collective bargaining to resolve differences between labor and management that have hitherto resulted in plant closure. The proposal put forth by Wendling mandates bargaining over the decision to close, but incorporates measures that will eliminate bargaining in circumstances where bargaining is not likely to lead to a solution. Furthermore, limits are placed on the length of time allowed for a resolution of differences in order to encourage good faith bargaining and achieve a solution that will maintain profitable operations and preserve jobs.

Facts and observations expressed in this study are the sole responsibility of the author. His viewpoints do not necessarily represent positions of the W. E. Upjohn Institute for Employment Research.

Robert G. Spiegelman
Director

May 1984

v

EXECUTIVE SUMMARY

The objective of this study is to answer the following questions. First, what is the potential for bargaining to alter the decision to close when continued operation is a reasonable alternative? Second, can bargaining over the effects of closure provide a reasonable opportunity for workers to mitigate some of the consequences? Third, have management and labor used formal contract negotiations to obtain protections and to develop solutions for workers and firms "at risk of closure?"

The question may be raised: Why the interest in collective bargaining as a tool to alleviate the plant closure problem? First, a significant proportion of closures takes place in unionized facilities. Whereas a survey of Fortune 500 firms determined that 52 percent of the establishments were unionized, 66 percent of the closings involved unionized establishments. Second, the reasons for closure cited in surveys and court cases tend to be amenable to resolution through collective bargaining. The above survey revealed that 21 percent of the respondents cited high labor costs, 17 percent listed price competition from lower cost labor, and 10 percent referred to crippling union work rules. Reasons for closure cited in court cases have included low productivity, high wages and inflexible work rules. Thus, there are a significant number of instances in which the reasons cited for closing are topics that have been and could be handled through the collective bargaining process.

The plant closure issue must be placed in perspective. It appears to be a relatively infrequent event. For example, the Bureau of National Affairs reported that in 1982, a year marked by a deep recession, there were 619 closures affecting 215,525 workers in the United States. Of these closures, 424 were manufacturing facilities and resulted in putting 146,900 employees out of work; but this represented approximately 1 percent of both the manufacturing facilities and the manufacturing workforce.

Given the nature of the reasons for closure and the magnitude of the problem, collective bargaining may be the most appropriate institution to solve the problem. Collective bargaining can address the specific issues in a plant and may be able to tailor a solution that meets the needs of both parties, management and labor. Legislation cannot possibly accommodate all of the varied circumstances in which closure is considered.

To understand and evaluate the role that collective bargaining could play, both the case law that has evolved in the formulation of the judicial interpretations and the actual contract provisions negotiated in major collective bargaining agreements are examined. Furthermore, several rules and procedures which have been proposed to facilitate the determination of whether there is a duty to bargain over the decision are analyzed.

The examination of the judicial interpretation of the duty to bargain has found several troublesome areas. First, substantive labor law has been formulated regarding plant closure based on cases in which the parties to the dispute had not negotiated a formal contract. The closure occurred almost on the heels of the union winning the representation election. Thus, a determination has been made on the efficacy of collective bargaining resolving an issue even though the parties have never bargained. In fact, the most recent U.S. Supreme Court ruling on this issue occurred in *First National Maintenance Corporation v. National Labor Relations Board,* a case in which the parties did not have an established bargaining relationship.

Second, there has been the overriding concern with the terminology used in cases of displacement, rather than with the outcome. For example, subcontracting has been differentiated from replacing existing employees with independent contractors. The outcome has been the same, the process very similar, but the duty to bargain over the decision differs. A similar demarcation has occurred between plant closure and relocation.

Formal collective bargaining already occurs over plant closure, or at least over provisions to minimize the effects of closure. The results of the econometric analysis of major collective bargaining agreements has determined that workers at risk are not necessarily obtaining these protections. Variation in closure rates by industry is not a significant determinant of variations in contractual outcomes. Instead, the regression estimates show that the contractual outcomes are less sensitive to changes in employment and instead more dependent on the bargaining power of the union.

Due to the confusion created by the case law and the lack of consistency in the determinants of outcomes of formal negotiations, amending the

National Labor Relations Act's definition of mandatory topics of bargaining under "terms and other conditions of employment" to include bargaining over the decision to close may be one policy alternative for the plant closure dilemma. There are positive and negative aspects to this approach. One positive feature is that coverage would be uniform throughout the United States. A negative feature is that the National Labor Relations Act covers only those plants and workplaces where employees have elected a bargaining agent. Since plant closure is not restricted to unionized plants, protection will not be afforded in all instances.

This monograph contains a new proposal. Specifically, the proposal assumes that plant closure is a mandatory topic of bargaining. Steps are incorporated that ensure that actual bargaining occurs only in those instances in which there is a real probability that bargaining could lead to a solution. However, in no instance would more than 90 days elapse between the notice of closure and resolution of the situation, be it either a new agreement permitting continued operations or closure of the plant.

Neither management not labor have perfect foresight. Formal negotiations every two or three years cannot accommodate all contingencies. Equity considerations suggest that workers be afforded the opportunity to minimize earnings and/or job loss. Recognizing that doing so also imposes costs on employers, the proposal has been structured to be flexible and to expedite the bargaining process.

CONTENTS

Chapter 1   Introduction

I am fully aware that in this era of automation and onrushing technological change, no problems in the domestic economy are of greater concern than those involving job security and employment stability.
(Statement by Justice Potter Stewart in *Fibreboard Paper Products Corporation v. National Labor Relations Board* (85 S. Ct. 398, 411 (1964)).

The scope of public policy relating to plant closure and to those workers who are displaced is still unresolved. Should something more be done for the employees or required of the employer after a facility closes? Before it closes? Are the effects of closure mainly short term and corrected by the market? Are there long term consequences? Could collective bargaining play a greater role in solving this problem?

There are three ways in which collective bargaining may mitigate the problems associated with plant closure. First, judicial interpretations of the National Labor Relations Act have held that the employer must negotiate with the union over the effects of a decision to close a plant ("effects bargaining"). Second, although the decision by the United States Supreme Court in *First National Maintenance Corporation v. National Labor Relations Board* (101 S. Ct. 2573 (1981)) held that a firm need not bargain with the union over the decision to close one plant of a multiple plant operation ("decision bargaining"), this avenue has not been closed completely due to limitations in the opinion. For example, relocating one operation of a firm may require decision bargaining. Third, a union and employer may use the formal collective bargaining process to negotiate contract provisions

1

covering plant closure. Advance notice, severance pay and transfer rights are examples of these types of provisions.

The objective of this monograph is to answer the following questions. First, what is the potential for bargaining to alter the decision to close when continued operation is a reasonable alternative? Second, can bargaining over the effects of closure provide a reasonable opportunity for workers to mitigate some of the consequences? Third, have management and labor used formal contract negotiations to obtain protections and to develop solutions for workers and firms "at risk of closure?"

Plant closure is of significant legislative interest. The States of Maine and Wisconsin and the City of Philadelphia have enacted legislation that prescribes necessary action by firms to close a plant, and 17 other states had legislation on this issue formally introduced in their legislative sessions between 1979 and 1981 (McKenzie and Yandle 1982). California and Illinois adopted programs in 1982 to assist workers affected by plant closure and Rhode Island has established a special commission to study the problems caused by plant closure (Nelson 1983). In 1983, the States of Alabama, Connecticut and New York also acted to assist workers displaced by shutdowns or relocations (Nelson 1984). In addition, at least four proposals have been introduced in the United States Congress in previous sessions and the National Employment Priorities Act (H.R. 2847) was introduced in the 1983 session. Finally, employee stock ownership plans to purchase establishments have been facilitated by legislation and have been used to avert closure (Stern, Wood and Hammer 1979). In fact, Wintner (1983) reports that of approximately 60 employee buyouts, ony 2 have failed, and approximately 50,000 jobs have been preserved through this process.

Aside from the legislative interest in plant closure, the topic is of policy interest because it raises several complex philosophical questions about the course and control of economic activity. First, there is the question of whether the rights of owners of physical capital should take precedence over the rights of owners of human capital. Are firms and workers equally positioned to respond to economic change? Second, there is the conflict between equity and efficiency. Is it necessary that individuals suffer earnings losses so that corporations can maximize profits? Conversely, the mobility of workers and capital are both considered to enhance efficiency, but should restrictions be placed on the latter and not the former? Finally, there is the role of government policy. If government policies and actions increase the probability of closing a plant, can or should government policy be neutral towards the effects of closure?[1]

One such philosophical question arises when examining the unequal ability of firms and workers to respond to economic change (Martin 1983). For instance, a firm may make a capital investment in an industry. Due to changing market conditions, however, the firm recognizes that its future financial health is at stake unless it diversifies or changes markets. The firm redirects its resources and invests in a new activity, all of which may be done while it is still engaged in the original enterprise. In addition, the firm's new investment may be eligible for favorable tax treatment.

The situation facing the worker is quite different. The worker also invests in the firm through the accumulation of firm-specific skills. Assuming the worker recognizes that continued investment in the firm does *not* prevent displacement, he/she faces considerable difficulties in repositioning and diversifying his/her human capital. Time is required to develop new human capital before it can be sold in new markets, whereas the old human capital cannot be sold as scrap in a secondary market. Furthermore, investments to broaden one's human capital are not given special tax treatment, whereas investments to deepen it—such as investing more in one's current obsolete skill—are considered tax deductible. Since diversification may be necessary to minimize the impact of displacement, firms and workers are unequally positioned to respond to economic change.

However, it is necessary to place the plant closure issue in perspective. What is the magnitude of the plant closure problem? Since no governmental agency is charged with recording the closing of a plant or counting the number of workers directly affected, the exact magnitude of the plant closure problem is unknown. Consequently, several researchers have used auxiliary data to infer the extent of closure or have attempted to count the number of closures and workers impacted.

Bluestone and Harrison (1982) and Birch (1979) have used the Dun & Bradstreet data, which are actually collected to develop credit profiles of firms, to estimate the incidence of closures, start-ups and relocations. The Bureau of National Affairs (1983) has begun to tabulate the number of closings, but uses a combination of newspaper clippings, union reports and informed sources to develop their count of closures and affected workers. Schmenner (1982) has assembled data on the number of plant closures in the 1970s by surveying Fortune 500 firms.

Bluestone and Harrison's analysis of the Dun & Bradstreet data indicated that of every 10 manufacturing plants employing more than 100 workers open in 1969, 3 had closed by 1976. They also showed that the incidence of closure across the four major regions of the United States was quite similar during this time period (see table 1.1). In fact, the North Central region, which stretches from Ohio to North Dakota, had the lowest incidence of closure (25 percent) and the South, which ranges from Maryland to Oklahoma, had the highest incidence of closure (34 percent).

Table 1.1
Incidence of Closure by Region
Among Manufacturing Plants Employing More Than 100 Employees
From 1969 and 1976

Region	Number of states	Number of plants in 1969 sample	Number in sample closed by 1976	Incidence of closure of 1969 plants by 1976
Northeast	9	4,576	1,437	.31
North Central	12	3,617	904	.25
South	16	3,101	1,042	.34
West	13	1,155	344	.30
TOTAL	50	12,449	3,727	.30

SOURCE: Barry Bluestone and Bennett Harrison, *The Deindustrialization of America* (New York: Basic Books, Inc., 1982, Table 2.2).

Birch (1979) provided closure information on service establishments, which is presented in table 1.2. Although plant closure research has tended to emphasize manufacturing facilities, the service sector has grown in importance to the economy over the past two decades. Also, the impact of closure on individuals is not likely to vary significantly just because it is a service establishment and not a manufacturing facility. Furthermore, two of the three key U.S. Supreme Court decisions pertaining to the "duty to bargain over the decision to close a plant" have involved service operations.

The data shown in table 1.2 indicate a relatively high rate of closure among large service establishments, and a rate that is quite uniform across regions. Thus, the implication from these two tables is that the closure of firms is not simply a regional phenomena, but is prevalent throughout the United States.

Another approach to counting the number of displaced workers is to consider the population at risk. Risk can be evaluated along several dimensions; industry, occupation, age, region or tenure on the job are valid criteria. Alternatively, severity of unemployment can indicate a "risk group." For example, it most likely is a reasonable assumption that job losers who are associated with a declining industry are at risk of never getting back their positions and therefore of being displaced. Individuals who have been separated from their jobs for more than 26 weeks also have a diminishing probability of returning to their jobs.

The Congressional Budget Office (1982) has provided an estimate of the number of workers in January 1983 who are at risk of being displaced. Job losers were categorized along the dimensions listed above, with those meeting the criteria considered to be at risk. The results are provided in table 1.3.

The Bureau of National Affairs (1983) reported that there were 619 closures directly affecting 215,525 workers in 1982;

Table 1.2
Incidence of Closure by Region
Among Service Establishments Employing More Than 100 Employees
From 1969 and 1976

Region	Number of states	Number of establishments in 1969 sample	Number in sample closed by 1976	Incidence of closure of 1969 establishments by 1976
Northeast	9	633	237	.37
North Central	12	433	172	.40
South	16	476	182	.38
West	13	284	117	.41
TOTAL	50	1,826	708	.39

SOURCE: David Birch, *The Job Generation Process* (Cambridge, MA: M.I.T. Program on Neighborhood and Regional Change, 1979, Appendix D).

424 closures were manufacturing facilities and resulted in putting 146,900 employees out of work.[2] There were over 300,000 manufacturing establishments employing 18.8 million workers in 1982. Thus, slightly more than 1 percent of the manufacturing facilities and slightly less than 1 percent of the manufacturing workforce were affected.

Table 1.3
Estimates of Jobless Workers
at Risk of Displacement in January 1983
Under Alternative Eligibility Standards

Eligibility criteria	Number of workers (000s)
Declining industry	880
Declining occupation	1,150
More than 45 years of age	890
Declining industry and 45 or more years of age	205
Declining industry and other unemployed in declining area, and 45 or more years of age	395
Declining occupation and 45 or more years of age	280
More than 26 weeks of unemployment	560

SOURCE: Congressional Budget Office, *Dislocated Workers: Issues and Federal Options,* Washington, DC: U.S. Government Printing Office, 1982. This estimate, which is based on tabulations from the March 1980 Current Population Survey, also assumes that the number of displaced workers would not change between December 1981 and January 1983. Thus, these figures are conservative estimates of the actual figures.

Additional evidence on the incidence of plant closure is provided by Schmenner (1982) who collected closure data for the 1970s from Fortune 500 firms. During the 1970s, these firms closed approximately 8 percent of the plants that had been in existence at the start of the decade.[3] Although averages can be misleading, less than 1 percent of the existing plants of Fortune 500 firms were closed per year, a rate which is consistent with the BNA findings for 1982. The in-

cidence of plant closure by industry as tabulated by Schmenner is reported in table 1.4.

Table 1.4
Percentage of Plants Closed in Manufacturing Industries
in the 1970s by Fortune 500 Firms

Industry	Number of plants	Number closed	Percentage closed
Food & Kindred Products (20)	2,174	222	10.2
Tobacco Manufacturers (21)	32	1	3.1
Textile Mill Products (22)	383	36	9.4
Apparel (23)	267	24	9.0
Lumber & Wood Products (24)	401	30	7.5
Furniture & Fixtures (25)	183	23	12.6
Paper & Allied Products	907	60	6.6
Printing & Publishing (27)	258	15	5.8
Chemicals & Allied Products (28)	1,739	119	6.8
Petroleum Refining (29)	397	12	3.0
Rubber Products (30)	494	38	7.7
Leather & Leather Products (31)	80	16	20.0
Stone, Clay, Glass & Concrete Products (32)	648	44	6.8
Primary Metals Industries (33)	603	49	8.1
Fabricated Metal Products (34)	947	89	9.5
Machinery, Except Electrical (35)	1,056	75	7.1
Electrical Machinery (36)	965	85	8.8
Transportation Equipment (37)	607	37	6.1
Scientific Instruments (38)	326	23	7.1
Miscellaneous Manufacturing (39)	212	23	10.8
Totals	12,679	1,021	

SOURCE: Calculations based on computer printout provided by Roger Schmenner, August 16, 1983.
NOTE: Two digit SIC code in parentheses.

It is obvious that there are significant differences in the
estimates of the magnitude of the problem. The analysis based on the Dun & Bradstreet data clearly signals a much
higher rate of closure—over 4 percent of the plants closed
each year—than do the Bureau of National Affairs and the
Schmenner calculations, which indicate approximately 1 percent of the manufacturing plants are closed each year.

The relative accuracy of the estimates is more than an academic question because the magnitude of the problem conditions the potential policy responses. Although Schmenner and the Bureau of National Affairs are derived from independent sources, they appear to be consistent; consequently, these estimates will be accepted. Therefore, the analysis of this study will be based on the assumption that the closure of a manufacturing facility is a relatively infrequent event.

As the United States economy moves out of the recessionary conditions that have plagued it since late 1979, there may be a tendency to forget about plant closures and the dislocated workers. The number of closures and the ranks of the dislocated always swell during recessions, and the assumption may be that the economic recovery will solve the problem.

This viewpoint does not recognize that closure and dislocated workers are chronic problems. Some plants are going to be shut down even while the economy is in a period of sustained growth, and consequently, workers are always going to be dislocated. Incentives that operate to concentrate the impact of closure on the older worker, or the immobile, will continue during recovery as well as recession. Consumer demands also change through time. Some industries will be growing and others will be declining. Since the most efficient locations for producing the new products may not be the same as for the old products, and since the skills required may not be identical, this process of change usually will generate some dislocation.

A more concrete example of this process is offered by the research findings of Schmenner (1983). He determined that for major firms in the 1970s, the average age of a plant at closing was 19.3 years and the median age of closed plants was 15 years. Fully one-third of the plants that were closed were only six years old or less, and two-thirds of the plants were modern single-story structures. Thus, the existence of a new plant in a community is not a guarantee that the workforce will *not* be displaced by a plant shutdown in the near future. Furthermore, although the average size of all plants in his study was approximately 490 employees, the average employment size of plants opening in the 1970s was approximately 240 employees.

The question may be raised: Why the interest in collective bargaining as a tool to alleviate the problem of plant closure and dislocated workers? First, a significant proportion of closures takes place in unionized facilities. Whereas 52 percent of the facilities surveyed by Schmenner were unionized, 66 percent of the closings involved unionized facilities (Schmenner 1982). Second, the reasons cited for closure in surveys and in court cases tend to be amenable to resolution through collective bargaining. Schmenner's survey revealed that 21 percent of the respondents cited high labor rates, 17 percent listed price competition due to lower cost labor, and 10 percent indicated crippling union work rules. (Multiple responses were permitted.) Reasons cited in court cases have included low productivity, high wages, and inflexible work rules. Thus, there are a significant number of instances in which the reasons cited for closing are topics that have been and could be handled through the collective bargaining process.

Reich (1981) has argued that desired social goals could be achieved more efficiently through bargaining rather than regulation. Collective bargaining can address the specific problems of the plant and may be able to tailor a solution that meets the needs of all parties. Legislation cannot possibly accommodate all of the varied circumstances in which closure is being considered. Sometimes, the best solution for all would be the end of production. In other circumstances, changes in wages, operating procedures and the division of responsibilities would result in profitable operations and continued employment. (Wintner's (1983) study documented one situation in which a 25 percent cut in wages and changes in work rules were necessary to make the employee owned company competitive.) Furthermore, if collective bargaining could lead to profitable operations and continued employment, some older workers would not be faced with the prospect of seeking new employment while possessing outdated skills, nor would the economic impact on the community be as severe.[4]

The reasons listed above suggest that not only may the plant closure problem be amenable to mitigation through collective bargaining, but using collective bargaining may be more consistent with institutional and political considerations than direct regulation. Bacow (1980) has written that we need to be concerned with more than economic efficiency as we seek solutions to problems.

> If we are to develop a useful theory for matching tools to problems, then the criteria used for evaluating the match must reflect not only efficiency considerations, but also the managerial, institutional and political factors that determine the effectiveness of policies in practice (p. 132).

The other area of concern of this monograph relates to the labor market. Research on plant closure has paid little attention to the actual functioning of the labor market and whether the proposed policies are designed to correct market imperfections. Instead, it has tended to concentrate on one theme, the reemployment experience of dislocated workers. The method of analysis usually has been the case study. Based on this research, policies for alleviating the observed hardships associated with closure have been proposed.

Issues that have not been addressed or have been discussed only casually include the relationship between compensation schedules and estimates of earnings loss. Compensation schedules also could affect the structure of severance pay. An additional issue is the dichotomy between large local labor markets and small local labor markets. Another unresolved issue is whether compensating wage differentials exist for the positive probability of a plant closure.

The outline of this monograph is as follows. Chapter 2 addresses the functioning of the labor market in the presence of plant closure. Specific topics include: compensation schedules, estimates of earnings loss and the structure of severance pay; small and large local labor markets; and compensating wage differentials for the probability of plant closure. One other labor market issue, the impact of closure on older workers, is treated separately in Appendix A.

Chapter 3 is a discussion of the judicial interpretation of the duty to bargain over the decision to close and effects of closure. Also analyzed are the related issues of plant relocation and transfer of work. Chapter 4 discusses guidelines, rules and tests that have been proposed to facilitate the determination of a duty to bargain over the decision to close. An alternate proposal also is presented in this chapter. The empirical examination of the extent of bargaining over this issue is presented in chapter 5. The synthesis of the several aspects of this study and the conclusions are presented in the final chapter.

NOTES

1. Bluestone and Harrison (1980) asserted that the provisions of the tax code have provided indirect incentives to construct new facilities rather than rebuilding or renovating older facilities. These incentives include: (a) not treating land as a depreciable asset; (b) differential treatment of new and used facilities for purposes of accelerated depreciation; (c) tax credits that encourage the purchase of a newer vintage of tools and machinery; (d) tax deductibility of plant closure costs; (e) the special treatment of industrial development bonds; and (f) tax deductibility of many of the costs of homeownership.

2. Note that using the BNA calculation, the average numer of employees in the manufacturing facilities that closed was 348. The average number of employees in the typical manufacturing facility in the United States

was 63. Given that the BNA data set basically was collected by means of newspaper clippings, there may be a bias to their figures that understates the number of closures and overstates the average size of the closed facility. The closure of a smaller facility simply may not be reported.

The data on closure may be confused at times with business failures. For example, approximately 17,000 businesses failed in 1981. Business failures are defined as "concerns discontinued following assignment, voluntary or involuntary petition in bankruptcy, attachment, execution, foreclosure, etc.; voluntary withdrawals from business with known loss to creditors; also enterprises involved in court action, such as receivership and reorganization or arrangement which may or may not lead to discontinuance; and businesses making voluntary compromises with creditors out of court." (*United States, Statistical Abstract, 1982-1983.*) Thus, the definition of business failures is broader than that of plant closure which is the closing of a plant, establishment or company.

3. This calculation was based on information contained in a computer printout provided by Roger Schmenner to the author.

4. The role of collective bargaining in alleviating the plant closure problem was examined in more detail in late 1950s and early 1960s. Examples include the research of Killingsworth (1962) and Shultz and Weber (1966). At that time it was felt that "collective bargaining by itself cannot fully solve these problems." (Killingsworth, p. 210). Shultz and Weber wrote, "It has been asserted that collective bargaining cannot change the economic climate, that it can only ration the sunshine—or the rain as the case may be. . . . It should not be concluded, however, that collective bargaining has or will play only a minor role in adjustments to technological and economic change." (p. 46).

Chapter 2

The Functioning of the Labor Market

Introduction

Plant closure is considered a significant problem by some primarily because of the labor market impacts of its aftermath: earnings losses, long spells of unemployment, and altered career expectations. The public policy debate has revolved around whether direct policy interventions are required to correct these labor market impacts (Gordus, Jarley and Ferman 1981).[1] Naturally, there are different viewpoints as to the significance of the problem and whether any solution is possible that will actually improve and not worsen conditions in the long run.

Some recognize that dislocated workers are the victims of closure, but assert that no specific policy is necessary because *ex ante* and *ex post* protections are in place. Specifically, it is asserted that wages paid to workers contain a component which compensates workers *ex ante* for the differential probability of being displaced (McKenzie 1981). Furthermore, *ex post* protection is afforded for those losing their jobs, even as a result of plant closure, through unemployment compensation. Moreover, any attempt to alter the decision to close would impede the free movement of capital and lead to inefficient outcomes (McKenzie 1979).

Evidence used to support direct intervention includes the initial and long term earnings losses experienced by workers as a result of the closure (Jacobson 1979; Holen et al. 1981).

15

The increased incidence of physical and/or mental health impairment among the displaced also is used to argue for intervention (Kasl and Cobb 1979). Furthermore, there is the perspective that workers and firms are unequally positioned to diversify to meet changing economic circumstances (Martin 1983).

There also is considerable concern with the process of closure. Companies are thought to be acting irresponsibly and unfairly when profitable plants are closed because those resources can be invested more profitably elsewhere. A related issue is when plants are used as "cash cows": profits from the plant are not reinvested in that facility but are used elsewhere, and eventually the plant is closed. Reluctance to provide advance notice of the closure also is criticized (Blueston and Harrison 1980). Conversely, some adopt the stance that the decision to close is solely a management prerogative and intervention, such as bargaining with union representatives, is neither appropriate nor necessary.

As we consider the plant closure issue, the question we must attempt to address is: Assuming closure is a problem requiring a public policy initiative, how can policy be constructed so that its disruptive impact is limited, yet it is effective at correcting the problem? Therefore, it is important to investigate the functioning of the labor market in order to understand the basis of the undesirable effects and to determine if protections are in place and if they are adequate.

Three labor market issues will be addressed in this chapter. The first is the structure of compensation schedules, the resulting estimates of earnings loss and the equitable structure of severance pay. The second is the dichotomy between small and large local labor markets, with implications for the job search of displaced workers. The final one is the notion of equalizing differentials (*ex ante* adjustments) and its applicability to plant closure. Numerous other issues do influence the debate, but an exhaustive treatment of them is beyond the scope of this study.

Compensation Schedules, Earnings Loss and Severance Pay

The compensation schedules used by firms is not a topic that has generated significant policy interest. It is important in the case of plant closure, however, because the type of the compensation schedule may affect the estimate of the earnings loss and the structure of an equitable severance pay formula.

Lazear (1981) suggests that firms may design efficient compensation schedules in which workers do not receive a wage equal to the value of their marginal product (VMP). The usual assumption is that the wage of the worker should equal his/her marginal productivity times the price of the product.[2] Lazear contends that it pays for firms "to enter into long term wage-employment relationships which pay workers wage rates less than their VMP when they are junior, and more than their VMP when they are senior employees." (p. 607) The motivation of the employer for this schedule is that it should reduce shirking by workers and increase employee attachment to the firm because they will not receive the higher wages later on if they are terminated now.[3]

An example of the type of compensation schedule considered by Lazear is presented in figure 2.1. V(t) is a representation of a worker's value of marginal product over time. W't is the schedule of reservation wages for the worker, the minimum wage at which the worker will supply labor to the firm. W(t) is a wage schedule in which the present value of wages paid equals the present value of VMP, which is the schedule V(t). The worker beginning employment with the firm should be indifferent between being com-

pensated according to the wage path represented by either
V(t) or W(t). For purposes of analysis, we will use this
schedule as representative for the entire firm, such that different points along the horizontal axis represent workers
with different tenure.

Figure 2.1

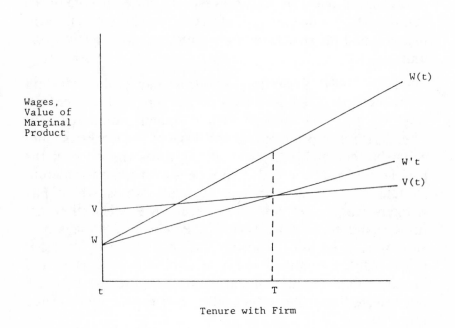

Implicit in this form of compensation is employment
through time T, which is the efficient date of retirement.[4] At
this tenure, the worker has been fully compensated for the
below VMP wages received earlier, and the value of his/her
work with this firm is less than the value of his/her time
away from this firm. However, if the employment contract is
broken prior to T, the worker has not been fully compen-

sated. Plant closure is one example of breaking an implicit contract. Thus, when this type of compensation schedule is used, an implicit obligation is created from the firm to the worker. The firm has "defaulted" to the worker because the worker has invested in the firm during the early stage of tenure by accepting a wage less than VMP with the expectation (condition) of being paid back by receiving a wage greater than VMP in the latter state of tenure with the firm.[5]

An examination of figure 2.1 indicates the nature of the earnings loss. If V(t) also represents the likely next best alternative in the labor market for the displaced worker, the initial earnings loss (L) will be: $L = W(t) - V(t)$. The earnings loss for more senior workers will be greater than the loss for less senior workers. This relationship is reasonably consistent with the findings of Holen et al. (1981) who determined that men under the age of 40 suffered a 13.4 percent drop in earnings in the first year after closure whereas men over the age of 40 suffered a 39.9 percent drop in earnings.[6]

The earnings loss of workers can be analyzed further, as is presented in figure 2.2. Assume the worker has been with the firm t* years when the plant closes. This worker's spot wage is exactly equal to his/her value of the marginal product. Given that s/he has been working with the firm since t, the worker has "invested" an amount equal to the area AVW, and the firm has implicitly agreed to pay back an amount equal to area ADE. Assuming that V(t) represents the next best employment opportunity, there is no immediate earnings loss.

Assume there is another worker whose tenure with the firm is t** years when the plant closes. Given the same circumstances as in the previous example, the initial earnings loss will be CB. The firm has borrowed the amount AVW, repaid area ABC, but still is in default area BCDE.

The more senior worker is likely to suffer the greater initial wage loss, but the lifetime earnings loss of the junior worker is significantly greater. The worker with tenure t* has not been paid area ADE, whereas the lifetime earnings loss of the worker with tenure t** is CBDE, which is the smaller amount.

Figure 2.2

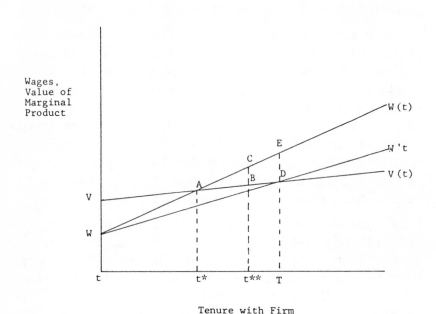

Tenure with Firm

This analysis of earnings loss is consistent with the estimates developed by Jacobson (1979). His analysis demonstrated that earnings losses over the course of the worker's lifetime rose as tenure in the job increased, reached a maximum at seven years of tenure, and then decreased with additional years of tenure. The principal reason for this finding is that those individuals with greater tenure also tend to have fewer years left in the labor force, and therefore the compounded effect tends to be smaller.

Thus, it is necessary to consider the two aspects of wage loss. There is the transitory wage loss which is the difference in the wage that one is able to obtain after closure relative to the previous wage. The second is the permanent earnings loss due to the interrupted work history, which changes the earnings profile. In addition, there is the wage loss due to a spell of unemployment that may follow closure.

The usual diagram of earnings loss is presented in figure 2.3. The distance MN in figure 2.3 corresponds to CB in figure 2.2, which is the transitory earnings loss. The usual estimate of earnings loss is the area of MNP, which corresponds to the loss incurred until the worker attains his/her former earnings. However, as Jacobson correctly points out, the real area of interest is MNQ, which measures both the transitory loss and the loss associated with a disrupted earnings schedule.

An additional point needs to be made in regards to figure 2.2. Suppose a worker is at tenure T when the facility closes. The measure of wage loss would be ED. However, the firm has no implicit obligation to the worker since it has fully repaid what it has borrowed. Conversely, the worker at t* would be judged to have suffered no immediate wage loss, although the lifetime earnings loss would be at a maximum. Therefore, examination of the differences in the wage received pre- and post-closure as a measure of policy necessity would lead to inappropriate judgments about instances in which there may be the need for remedial action.

The frequency of this type of compensation schedule is unknown. It may actually take the form of job ladders in which the marginal product expected increases less than the wage as one moves up the ladder. Furthermore, other implications arise from this type of schedule. For instance, it is likely that workers demand that wage schedules correspond more closely to the value of the marginal product in firms where it is anticipated that closure is more likely. Conversely, firms that are risky undertakings have the incentive to establish a schedule which deviates considerably from V(t).

Figure 2.3

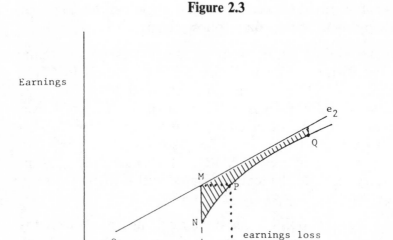

Earnings Losses Caused by Plant Closure

e_1 = expected earnings profile of workers without plant closure

e_2 = earnings of workers displaced by plant closure

c = time of closure

Although the measured earnings loss may be somewhat of an artifact of the compensation schedule, workers who have worked less than T years for this firm do indeed incur an earnings loss if their employment is terminated. Lazear has shown that a lump-sum payment is a mechanism to fully compensate a worker whose accumulated compensation is less than the accumulated value of his/her marginal product as the result of the termination of an employment contract. One form of a lump-sum payment is severance pay, which has been incorporated in plant closing legislative proposals.

Severance pay is the compensation given to a worker who is terminated. The connotation associated with it is that the leaving is involuntary and perhaps unexpected. For example, severance pay is given to workers who are excised whereas pensions are paid to workers who retire. The usual presumption is that severance pay is given to ease the pain and to tide the worker over until something new can be found following the involuntary separation. However, severance pay also can be used as an incentive, and as a form of deferred but earned compensation. Finally, severance pay can be used as a deterrent to closure. All four of these uses have direct bearing on the plant closure.

A key feature of the employment relationship is that both parties are bound by certain rules, obligations and expectations, with one expectation being continued employment. For instance, Hall (1982) determined that 51.1 percent of all men are likely to work 20 years or more for the same firm. When the expectation of continued employment is not met and where performance of the employee has been above certain prescribed levels, the implicit contract has been violated. To maintain respect for the implicit contract, a payment is made to the worker that indicates that management is ending the contract reluctantly.

The second role that the severance payment can play is that of an incentive. Consider the case of plant closure. As workers become aware that the plant is to close, they may engage in job search in order to find alternate employment. They may do this to get a head start on all the others who also will become involuntarily laid off or because they may be aware of specific opportunities.

Workers quitting in order to find other employment may not be in the best interest of the firm as it attempts to continue production until closing. Those with the best alternate employment opportunities also may be the most skilled. Thus management may offer an attractive severance pay schedule, but only to those workers who stay until the plant closes. In order to maintain the most skilled workers, who may also be the most experienced, the severance pay schedule is positively correlated with years of experience, such as two weeks of pay for every year of experience. In this situation, severance pay is an incentive to stay, but with a very real cost to the worker if s/he leaves before the plant is closed.

The third role that the severance payment can play is that of deferred but earned compensation (Lazear 1981, 1982) and Stoikov (1969). The conventional schedule for severance pay establishes it as a positive linear function of the number of years worked. For example, legislation proposed in Michigan sought the following form of severance payment. "The severance benefit shall be equal to the average weekly wage of the affected employee multiplied by the number of full and fractional years for which the employee has been employed."[7] Adopting Lazear's formulation, this proposal would not fully compensate workers for the deferred but unpaid compensation.

Examining figure 2.4, the conventional proposal envisions a severance pay schedule suggested by tAB. However, if one objective of severance pay is to fully compensate workers for the implicit obligation, the severance pay schedule should take the form of tAT. The tAT schedule would result in the severance paid to a worker who has T years of experience with the firm when the plant closes being the same as the payment to the person who retires normally: zero.[8]

Why would a firm use a compensation schedule such as this? The argument is that it would reduce shirking. Why would the firm concern itself with making a severance payment? Again, it is the importance of maintaining the implicit contract. Reneging on workers by leaving them with a compensation deficit would make it virtually impossible for firms to implement this type of schedule in the future. Firms would then have to devise an alternate method, which may be more costly, to police workers and to minimize shirking. Consequently, there are advantages for both the firm and employees associated with severance payments.

Figure 2.4

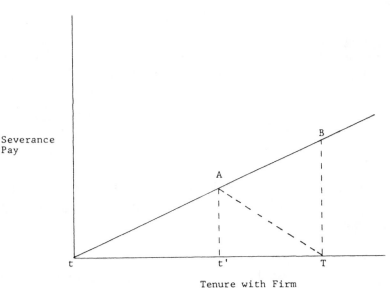

The fourth role of severance pay is to increase the cost of closing a plant such that closing may be the costlier alternative. This role seems most appropriate to the circumstance when the firm is considering relocating the operation. The firm must compare the cost of continuing operations at the old site with the sum of the costs of closing the old site and producing at the new site.

Consider the following simplified formulation. Define the cost of continuing operations at the old site as C_o, where

$$C_o = (\sum_{i=1}^{\infty} f_{io} + \sum_{i=1}^{\infty} W_{io})/(1+r)^i$$

and where

$\sum_{i=1}^{\infty} f_{io}/(1+r)^i$ is the discounted present value of future nonlabor factor of production at the old facility costs, and

$\sum_{i=1}^{\infty} W_{io}/(1+r)^i$ is the discounted present value of future labor costs at the old facility.

Define the cost of closing the old site and producing at the new site (over the same time horizon) as C_p, where

$$C_p = X_{co} + X_{cp} + S_{io} + W_{ipm} + (\sum_{i=1}^{\infty} W_{ip} + \sum_{i=1}^{\infty} f_{ip})/(1+r)^i,$$

and where

X_{co} is the fixed cost of closing down the old facility, and X_{cp} is the fixed cost of starting production at the new facility,

and

f_{ip} is the discounted present value of future nonlabor factor of production costs at the new facility, and

W_{ip} is the discounted present value of future labor costs at the new facility, and

S_{io} is the severance obligation to the workers at the old facility.

Obviously, relocation will not take place unless $C_p < C_o$; but $W_{ip} < W_{io}$ since fewer labor resources are likely to be used per unit of output. With regard to nonlabor factor of production costs, $f_{ip} \gtrless f_{io}$, since capital is being substituted for labor. Assuming $f_{ip} = f_{io}$, the problem becomes

$$\left[\left(\sum_{i=1}^{\infty} (W_{io} - W_{ip})/(1+r)^i \right) \right] > (X_{co} + X_{pn} + S_{io})$$

Therefore, as S_{io} is increased, it becomes more unlikely that wage savings at a new location outweigh the fixed costs of closure. Therefore, increasing the severance obligation of the firm raises the probability of $C_p > C_o$, which would make the relocation uneconomical.

It is obvious that there is a conflict between designing a severance pay schedule that fully compensates workers for deferred compensation and a schedule that imposes significant costs on a firm if it decides to close a plant. The pattern that closings appear to follow is that the actual closing is preceded by a significant length of time in which employment is reduced gradually. Due to seniority provisions incorporated into bargained contracts, those remaining at the time of closure are the most senior employees.

Consider a firm in which the following workers, categorized by years of experience, are employed and eligible for severance pay when closure is announced.

Years of Experience	Number of Workers	Total Severance Payment	
		Schedule A	Schedule B
20	20	$ 80,000	$ 4,000
15	15	45,000	15,000
10	10	20,000	20,000
5	5	5,000	5,000
	Total	$150,000	$44,000

Severance payments under Schedule A are calculated as two weeks of average pay for every year worked, where the average pay is $200 for two weeks. The formula for Schedule B is designed to compensate for deferred earnings. Consequently, two weeks of average earnings ($200) are payed for each year worked up to 10 years, at which time the schedule changes to $200 $(10 + (11 - t))$ for each year worked more than 10 years. T, the efficient retirement tenure, equals 21 years in this example. As can be seen, the severance payment owed by the firm under A ($150,000) is significantly greater than under B ($44,000), and therefore, Schedule A is much more likely to deter a closure.

Small Local Labor Markets
Versus Large Local Labor Markets

The key element in the plant closure debate is the reemployment experience of those workers who are displaced. Recognizing that the problem is one of scale, the public policy proposals have tended to include only firms employing more workers than some predetermined size. This approach, though, may ignore circumstances of the local labor market.

The concern is whether the local labor market approximates a perfectly competitive labor market. Are workers likely to have alternate employment opportunities in that area? Or are real alternatives going to require relocation to another labor market? Are wages going to be competitive, or does the closing of the one plant depress the labor market's wage level?

If the local market is relatively large, as evidenced by numerous employers and therefore numerous employment opportunities, the market may approximate the competitive model. No change of residence is necessary to access new opportunities; perhaps only changing commuting patterns is required. Furthermore, since there are many employers, no one employer can establish a wage scale. Numerous employment opportunities enforce the competitive setting of wages because if one employer deviates too far from the competitive wage, workers will leave and accept new employment opportunities.

A small local labor market may not approximate the perfectly competitive model. The local market may not provide the range of options necessary so that workers can change jobs without undue expense. Instead, job mobility may entail relocation to another labor market.[9] Furthermore, one employer may act as a monopsonist demander of labor, paying workers a lower wage than would be paid in a competitive market.[10] Jacobson (1979) determined that lifetime earnings losses resulting from a plant closure tend to be inversely related to the size of the local labor market.

Thus, the closure of a plant in a large local labor market may not require direct intervention because labor can be highly mobile among a number of alternatives. The incentive to bargain over the decision to close also may be limited due to the numerous options available. Relocation to find alternate employment is not as likely to be necessary. Conversely, if that same plant closed in a small community, relocation may be necessary. Specifically, the market will not function as hypothesized because the conditions necessary are not present. Workers in this circumstance may have a greater incentive to obtain relocation allowances through the collective bargaining contract, grant more concessions to keep the plant open, or as Wintner (1983) has shown, buy out the plant so that it can continue operating.

The difficulty is in developing an administrative framework for determining whether the conditions for a smooth functioning market are present or not. When is a closure a serious problem in a local labor market? The usual approach is to require firms with more than 50 or 100 employees to be subject to the statute. Obviously, the scope of the problem depends on the size of the local labor market.

The closure of a facility with 100 employees may be inconsequential in a community of 250,000, whereas it would be devastating in a community of 5,000.

This comparison would suggest that one approach might be to convert the numer of employees affected to a percentage of the local labor force. This also is problematic because the size of a facility can be a variable. The result could be that firms would not establish facilities that exceeded the percentage threshold. A notch would develop at this point; but this approach would be more acceptable than one that automatically covers all firms exceeding some size irrespective of the conditions in the local labor market.

Compensating Wage Differentials
(*Ex Ante* Payments)

The theory of compensating differentials was introduced by Adam Smith who observed that some types of jobs required greater compensation than others because the work had certain undesirable characteristics associated with it such as greater hazards or frequent interruptions of employment. If the theory of compensating wage differentials applies to plant closure, workers employed in firms in which there is greater likelihood of permanent closure would receive a compensating differential as part of their wage (an *ex ante* payment) . That differential would make their expected compensation in that firm equal to the compensation they would receive in a firm with more stable employment prospects, everything else being equal. If this is the case, the affected workers would require no additional policy consideration because they already have been fully compensated by the firm. McKenzie (1981) asserts that workers are so compensated.

Baily (1974) utilizes this theory in devising wage and employment strategies for firms. He writes, "To attract workers, the firm must pay a higher wage if there is some positive probability of unemployment than it would if employment were guaranteed'' (p. 38). Abowd and Ashenfelter (1981) found evidence of compensating differentials for workers in industries in which layoffs were anticipated. Holding other factors constant, they found that the value of the differential was directly proportional to the extent of anticipated unemployment.

There are a number of questions relating to the relevance of the theory of compensating wage differentials to plant closure. First, is the permanent layoff resulting from plant closure anticipated unemployment? Baily (1977) wrote that workers ''are assumed to have an expectation about the layoff policy of the firm. . . . This assumption is appropriate where firms have a history of hiring and firing: a pattern or reputation for the firm is established.'' Differentials result from accumulated knowledge, but the reputation developed from plant closure cannot be applied by the workers to the specific experience because there is no future employment opportunity with that firm in the local labor market. That is, there is no opportunity to recontract with the firm. There is, however, the opportunity to recontract with another firm in the same industry.

Second, in the theory of compensating wage differentials, how do workers obtain information about an attribute of the workplace or the firm? For example, an employee can observe the degree of workplace hazards and attempt to obtain a new wage reflecting those conditions. However, information about plant closure has been so scarce and fragmented, as is evident from chapter 1, that it is difficult to envision reliable estimates of the differential probability of closing. Schmenner's (1983) analysis, which found one-third of closures being of plants less than six years old, suggests that a large element of closure is random, which makes estimating the necessary differential very tenuous. Since the policy interest in this issue is leading to more data being collected, more reliable probabilities of closure may be developed in the future.

Summary

Casual observation of labor market outcomes pre- and post-closure may provide a distorted view of the earnings losses of workers. The tendency to emphasize initial losses rather than permanent losses concentrates attention on the older worker when, in fact, the worker in the middle of his career may be most severely impacted because the interrupted work history decreases the expected lifetime earnings profile.

The local labor market is a key determinant of the impact of closure on workers. Jacobson found earnings losses associated with plant closure to be inversely related to the size of the local labor market. Policies that do not recognize these differences may be onerous in some instances and inadequate in others, which suggests that the policy approach needs to be flexible so that it can be adapted to the local circumstances.

Finally, the theory of compensating differentials probably does not hold in the case of plant closure. The inability to recontract with a closed firm coupled with the difficulty of obtaining reliable estimates of the differential probability of closure make it unlikely that *ex ante* protection is afforded workers. One possibility is to encourage recontracting with a firm that has a high probability of closing.

In conclusion, because the impact of closure depends on the specific circumstances of the workers, the firm and the labor market, a uniform policy may be successful in some instances and deleterious in others. Collective bargaining, which by its nature is flexible and sensitive to local conditions, may be a socially acceptable way to make adjustments to some labor market outcomes.

NOTES

1. There have been two major types of plant closure policy initiatives. The first has been to prescribe the behavior of firms intending to close. Advance notice, continued wage payments, and severance payments to workers and communities are elements of this type of initiative. In some respects, the purpose of these requirements has been to make closure so onerous that firms would not carry through with a threat of closure. The second type has been to develop assistance programs for those workers displaced including job clubs, retraining, job search skills and relocation. This approach has been adopted more frequently by individual states, since it has been thought that the more prescriptive types of governmental action would place a state at a competitive disadvantage for economic development purposes.

2. The reader will note that according to the economic theory, the wage only equals the value of the marginal product of the last person hired. This assumes that workers are homogeneous and are working with a fixed and identical capital stock. However, there are different job ladders within a firm, employees have different responsibilities and they are not necessarily working with the same capital, which requires deviations in compensation. Lazear's analysis addresses the long run compensation schedule within the firm.

3. Lazear develops the model further by demonstrating that firms will develop compensation schedules that are of this shape, but the present value of $W(t)$ is greater than that of $V(t)$. When the earnings stream is greater than the productivity stream, the cost of shirking to the employee increases, so the compensation schedule essentially becomes a policing mechanism. His analysis has other interesting implications for plant closure, but our present concern is with the implications of this schedule for the measurement of earnings loss.

4. Abraham and Medoff (1983) assert that a deferred compensation schedule requires that the relative protection against job loss also grows with length of service so that firms are not permitted to terminate workers once wages exceed VMP. In fact, they found that written provisions specifying seniority as an important determinant of layoff priority are associated with a reduction in the vulnerability of senior workers losing their jobs.

5. Lazear (p. 609) describes this process as follows: The firm has defaulted "since the firm essentially is borrowing from the worker by

paying him less than VMP when he is young and repaying him by paying more than the VMP when old.''

The relationship of the shape of the earnings profile to the shape of the value of the marginal product schedule also is an interesting issue. One set of possible wage paths would be as depicted in figure 2.5.

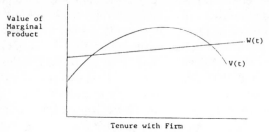

This approach is flawed by the fact that anytime the worker's V(t) exceeds W(t) paid by the firm, there is the incentive to leave the firm. A firm would not adopt this type of schedule because (a) it does not reduce shirking, and (b) it does not increase employee attachment. Thus, although one can envision the situation in which the worker is in debt to the firm, particularly when there is significant firm-specific training, this type of schedule does not satisfy any of the motivations of the firm.

6. The initial earnings loss is not strictly a result of Lazear's formulation. For instance, Wachter and Wascher (1983) use a more general age-earnings profile and also derive an immediate wage loss that is the difference between the wage paid and the opportunity wage. Furthermore, in their formulation, the early wage with the firm is less than the opportunity wage. The distinction is that their age-earnings profile is the result of job-specific human capital. The implications of this profile may differ, however, and depend on the financing of the job-specific training.

7. This wording is taken from Substitute for House Bill No. 4330 "A Bill to Provide for Community Preservation and Recovery After an Employer Closes, Relocates or Reduces Its Operation." (1981)

8. Of course this ignores the role that pension payments play as deferred compensation.

9. Baily (1974) incorporates mobility costs in his model of wage and employment variation. He stresses the role that mobility costs play in the decision to change jobs and that mobility costs vary by training and the local labor market.

10. A perfectly competitive market also is a precondition for payment of an equalizing differential.

Chapter 3

The Duty to Bargain
Judicial Interpretations

Introduction

The National Labor Relations Act (NLRA) was enacted into law in 1935. It forms the basis of the legal framework for collective bargaining in the private sector in the United States. An administrative agency, the National Labor Relations Board (NLRB) is charged with administering the terms of the NLRA.

The National Labor Relations Act provides for the right of workers to organize and select a representative to serve as their exclusive bargaining agent. The Act also imposes "a mutual obligation of the employer and representative of the employees to meet at reasonable times and confer in good faith with respect to wages, hours and other terms and conditions of employment."[1] Because Congress did not specify what constitutes "other terms and conditions" in detail, there has been considerable uncertainty as to what actions and practices are covered by these words.

"Wages, hours and other terms and conditions of employment" are mandatory topics of bargaining. They cannot be changed unilaterally by either party to the collective bargaining contract. Mandatory topics must be negotiated to impasse. If unilateral changes are made prior to impasse, an unfair labor practice is committed. However, it is in the case-by-case determination of whether an unfair labor practice has been committed that the NLRB, the Circuit Court of Appeals and the United States Supreme Court have decided what actions and practices are mandatory topics of bargaining.

The evolving case law of collective bargaining over plant closure increasingly has changed the economic considerations brought into the analysis. Arguments supporting no duty to bargain over the decision to close have moved from the right of management to run its business as it sees fit (the core of entrepreneurial control),[2] to whether the reasons are primarily economic in nature,[3] to whether the economic reasons are amenable to change through collective bargaining.[4] Furthermore, the concepts discussed have advanced to include not only the capital investments by the owners of the firm, but also to include the human capital investments made by the employees.[5]

The implicit assertion in the former arguments is that economic efficiency is maximized when the use and movement of physical capital is unconstrained (McKenzie 1979). The implicit contention in the latter arguments is that strict economic efficiency ignores those costs which are borne by others as a result of the firm's action—the social costs—and considers only those costs borne by the firm (Coase 1971). Consequently, what is efficient for the firm may not be efficient for society.

Bargaining over the decision to close a plant presumably could incorporate both private and social costs in the decision calculus so that a socially efficient decision could be reached. Conversely, bargaining is not costless. Imposing a duty to bargain over the decision to close in all partial closure circumstances could result in a socially inefficient solution if the extra bargaining costs exceed the benefits from bargaining.

There are two types of noncontract bargaining over plant closure: decision bargaining and effects bargaining. According to the interpretation of the United States Supreme Court, there is no duty to bargain over the decision of the owner to close down the entire operation of a firm.[6] Recently, it was established that there is no duty to bargain over the decision to close one plant (facility) of a multiple plant (facility) operation,[7] but there is a duty to bargain over the effects of closure.

The labor law concerning the duty to bargain over the decision to partially close an operation has been described as a conundrum (Heinsz 1981). This description is most apt. The law generally has recognized that the owners of firms place their capital and their livelihood at risk, and should be free to take the actions necessary to protect their investment and to generate a satisfactory return. However, the law also is cognizant that employees also place their human capital and livelihood at risk when joining a firm. To some this conflict between physical capital and human capital may be an issue of equity versus efficiency. Thus, it is to be expected that the National Labor Relations Board and the Circuit Court of Appeals have reached different conclusions on whether "the mutual obligation of the employer and the representative of the employees to meet at reasonable times and confer in good faith with respect to wages, hours and other terms and conditions of employment"[8] also includes bargaining over partial closure of operations.

The United States Supreme Court, in its ruling in *First National Maintenance Corporation v. National Labor Relations Board* (101 S. Ct. 2573 (1981)), did not totally resolve the issue.[9] The Supreme Court held there was no duty to bargain over the decision to close one part of an operation under the National Labor Relations Act. However, even the Supreme Court's majority opinion states as limitations that (a) First National Maintenance Corporation "had no intention to replace the discharged employees or to move the operations elsewhere,"[10] and (b) the "union was not selected as the bargaining representative until well after the petitioner's economic difficulties had begun."[11] Thus, the union was not the source of the financial difficulties, nor could it be expected that the union could effect changes to alleviate the difficulties.

Justice Stewart wrote almost two decades ago in his concurring opinion in *Fibreboard Paper Products Corporation v. National Labor Relations Board* (85 S. Ct. 398, 411 (1964)) that "no problems in the domestic economy are of greater concern than those involving job security and employment stability." This statement probably has never been more appropriate than now. The economy of the United States has been undergoing a gradual structural shift and back-to-back recessions have exacerbated the perceived decline. Perhaps most important, the plant closure problem will not go away during a sustained economic upturn. Schmenner (1983) has determined that there is a long run process underway in which manufacturing will be shifting from larger establishments to smaller ones.

This chapter examines the efficiency and equity arguments associated with the judicial interpretations of the duty to bargain over the decision to close or relocate a part of an enterprise. It usually is argued that the unfettered movement of capital is necessary to achieving economic efficiency. The most efficient allocation of resources occurs when capital is free to move to its most profitable use. But a related question should concern the investment in human capital. Would this investment be less than optimum when workers are experiencing frequent earnings losses due to closure? Will there be a reluctance to undertake firm-specific training?

Although the profit maximization motive leads to the most efficient allocation of resources, there is the recognition that some redistribution may take place. The implicit assumption is that the redistribution is among firms—that some will gain at the expense of others. However, these are potential equity implications of the redistribution involved in plant closure or relocation. Specifically, because firms are able to diversify and reposition more easily than workers, the firm may be maximizing profits at the expense of earnings losses of its workers.

The following review of the case law provides the institutional framework and the background arguments opposing and supporting the duty to bargain. Based on these it may be possible to establish a *per se* rule—the assignment of rights—that will result in maximizing the production of goods and services given that social costs are accommodated. The next chapter examines alternate *per se* rules that have been proposed to solve this conundrum and puts forth a new proposal.

Judicial Interpretations

The conundrum surrounding the duty to bargain over plant closure has resulted from the conflicting decisions that have been rendered by the National Labor Relations Board, the Circuit Court of Appeals and the United States Supreme Court. The cases have been decided by relying on different sections of the National Labor Relations Act. Specifically, the National Labor Relations Board has emphasized Section 8(a)5 which defines the refusal to bargain collectively with the elected representatives of the employees as an unfair labor practice. The Courts, by and large, have stressed defining the actions and activities that fall under the definition of other terms and condition of employment (Section 8(d)). Consequently, competing interpretations exist.

The question of bargaining over the decision to close a plant, to subcontract work or to move work from one plant to another hinges on whether the practice falls within the definition of wages, hours and other terms and conditions of employment. If it does, then it is a mandatory topic of negotiation. However, just because it is a mandatory topic does not mean that agreement must be reached. Instead, there simply must be an attempt at good faith bargaining. The first case presented here (*Borg-Warner*) established this principle. The following cases deal specifically with plant closure, subcontracting and movement of work issues, and whether negotiations occur during the course of a contract or while bargaining over a new contract. The description of the judicial developments below is not an exhaustive examination of all the cases pertaining to the interpretations of the duty to bargain. Other studies, such as Swift (1974), Heinsz (1981) and Miscimarra (1983) have already provided these.

National Labor Relations Board v. Wooster Division of Borg-Warner Corporation
(78 S. Ct. 718) (1958)

The United States Supreme Court decided this case in 1958. The crux of the case was the distinction between the duty to bargain over mandatory topics as opposed to permissive topics.

Borg-Warner Corporation attempted to include two clauses in the collective bargaining contract it was negotiating with the United Automobile, Aircraft and Agricultural Implement Workers of America (UAW), the certified representative of the employees. One was the "ballot" clause which would require a prestrike secret vote of all employees on the company's last offer. If the employees reject the offer, the company would have the opportunity to amend the final offer. The other provision was a "recognition" clause which was an attempt to exclude the International Union of the UAW and recognize only the UAW local as the bargaining representative.

The union rejected both ballot and recognition clauses saying each was totally unacceptable. Conversely, Borg-Warner Corporation indicated that no agreement would be reached unless it contrained both of these clauses. After a strike, the union gave in and signed an agreement incorporating both clauses. The International Union filed unfair labor charges with the National Labor Relations Board citing unfair labor practices within the meaning of Section 8(a) (5).

The Supreme Court analyzed Section 8(a) (5), which defines refusal to bargain collectively with the representatives of the employees, and Section 8(d), which requires bargaining over "wages, hours and other terms and conditions of employment." The Supreme Court indicated that the duty to bargain is limited to the subjects of wages, hours and other terms and conditions of employment. Furthermore, bargaining can take place over other issues, but at the discretion of each of the parties.

Mr. Justice Burton wrote what has become the definitive rule on bargaining rights and obligations surrounding mandatory and permissive topics of bargaining.

> But that good faith does not license the employer to refuse to enter into agreements on the ground that they do not include some proposal which is not a mandatory subject of bargaining. We agree with the Board that such conduct is, in substance, a refusal to bargain about the subjects that are within the scope of mandatory bargaining. This does not mean that bargaining is to be confined to statutory subjects. Each of the two controversial clauses is lawful in itself. Each would be enforceable if agreed to by the unions. But it does not follow that, because the company may propose these clauses, it can lawfully insist upon them as a condition to any agreement.[12]

Fibreboard Paper Products Corporation v. National Labor Relations Board
(85 S. Ct. 398 (1964))

The United States Supreme Court decided *Fibreboard* in 1964. The facts of the case were as follows. Just prior to the expiration of the collective bargaining agreement, Fibreboard Paper Products Corporation indicated to the union that substantial savings could be realized by contracting out the maintenance work at the expiration of the collective bargaining agreement. Prior to the next meeting with the union, which was to take place the day before the contract expired, Fibreboard engaged a firm to do the maintenance work. The company stated that further negotiations on a new agreement would be pointless. Formal negotiations between Fibreboard and the union, the United Steelworkers of America, had existed since 1937.

On appeal, the United States Supreme Court ruled that

> . . . on the facts of this case, the 'contracting out' of work previously performed by members of an existing bargaining unit is a subject about which the National Labor Relations Act requires employers and the representatives of their employees to bargain collectively. We also agree with the Court of Appeals that the Board did not exceed its remedial powers in directing the Company to resume its maintenance operations, reinstate the employees with back pay, and bargain with the Union.[13]

The bases for the decision of the majority were that (a) contracting out falls within the literal meaning of "terms and conditions of employment," (b) the industrial peace was likely to be promoted through the negotiation of the issue, and (c) the industrial practices of the United States indicated frequent negotiations over the issue of subcontracting. Furthermore, the changes being considered by the company involved no capital investment. It simply was a case of one set of workers being substituted for the company's employees.

The Supreme Court's majority opinion also addressed the issue of the likely success of negotiations settling the dispute. They wrote, "As the Court of Appeals pointed out, (i)t is not necessary that it be likely or probable that the union will yield or supply a feasible solution but rather that the union be afforded an opportunity to meet management's legitimate complaints that its maintenance was unduly costly."[14]

Justice Stewart's concurring opinion, however, became more influential than the majority opinion. Justice Stewart narrowed the scope of the decision by suggesting that the Court's decision was not a general rule, but only applied to the facts of this case—replacement of bargaining unit workers with others doing the same work in the same location. Only under circumstances such as these would the employer be required to bargain with the union over the decision to terminate the activity.

Justice Stewart limited the majority's opinion by stating that

> . . . it surely does not follow that every decision which may affect job security is a subject of compulsory collective bargaining. . . . An enterprise may decide to invest in labor saving machinery. Another may resolve to liquidate its assets and go out of business. Nothing the Court holds today should be understood as imposing a duty to bargain collectively regarding such managerial decisions, which lie at the core of entrepreneurial control. Decisions concerning the commitment of investment capital and the basic scope of the enterprise are not themselves primarily about conditions of employment, though the effect of the decision may be necessarily to terminate employment.[15]

National Labor Relations Board
v. Adams Dairy, Inc.
(322 F.2d 553) (1963)

The United States Court of Appeals for the Eighth Circuit decided this case in 1963. The facts of the case were as follows. Adams Dairy employed driver-salesmen and also engaged independent contractors to distribute their products. The driver-salesmen were members of a union that had negotiated formal agreements with Adams Dairy since 1954. In the course of negotiating a new contract, the employer expressed concern about the relative costs of the delivery service. A new contract was executed, however, without specifically addressing the costs of delivery service.

After the contract was signed, the employer initiated new discussions concerning its unfavorable competitive situation due to these higher costs. No specific proposals were introduced, nor was it indicated that the driver-salesmen would be terminated if no accord was reached. Subsequently, while the contract was still in force, Adams Dairy substituted independent contractors for its own driver-salesmen and terminated these employees.

The question was: Is the decision to terminate distribution of one's product a subject of mandatory bargaining under the provisions of the National Labor Relations Act? The Court began their analysis by asserting that "union membership is not a guarantee against legitimate or justifiable discharge or discharge motivated by economic necessity."[16] The Court also indicated that intent, motivation and natural consequences cannot be ignored when determining whether an unfair labor practice has been committed.

The Court held that the decision to terminate was not a mandatory topic of bargaining because the substitution of independent contractors for the driver-salesmen was made for legitimate business reasons. The intent and motivation was not to destroy the union, as evidenced by the fact that they had attempted to negotiate with the employees on previous occasions concerning an adjustment of the commission payments. The rest of the Court's ruling also is very significant. Specifically, they wrote: "After that decision had been made, however, Section 8(a) (5) did require negotiation with reference to the treatment of the employees who were terminated by the decision."[17] Thus, the United States Court of Appeals for the Eighth Circuit affirmed the concept of "effects" bargaining.

In placing this case in perspective, it is important to recall that the employer had attempted to negotiate with the driver-salesmen concerning the commission payments. When no relief was forthcoming, they substituted the independent contractors for the driver-salesmen. Therefore, they had established that this was a legitimate concern of their business and that if an accommodation could have been reached with the driver-salesmen, no change would have been made in employment.

Textile Workers Union of America v. Darlington Manufacturing Company et al., and National Labor Relations Board v. Darlington Manufacturing Company, et al.
(85 S. Ct. 994) (1965)

The United States Supreme Court decided this case in 1965. The Textile Workers Union successfully organized the workers of the Darlington Manufacturing Company in September of 1956. The Board of Directors met several days later and decided to liquidate the Darlington Manufacturing Company. The plant ceased operations in November and all equipment was sold in December. It was determined in the proceedings that the owner (Deering Milliken) of Darlington Manufacturing Company also operated 16 other textile manufacturers.

The issues to be adjudicated were the following. First, was Darlington Manufacturing Company a separate manufacturer or part of the entire Deering Milliken enterprise? Second, does a company have the right to close part or all of its business regardless of its motives? The Supreme Court implicitly held that Darlington Manufacturing Company was a separate company. It explicitly ruled: "We hold that so far as the Labor Relations Act is concerned, an employer has the absolute right to terminate his entire business for any reason he pleases, but disagree with the Court of Appeals that such right includes the ability to close a part of a business no matter what the reason."[18]

In developing its opinion, the Supreme Court asserted the primacy of decisions based on sound economic reasons as opposed to those with a discriminatory motive. Those decisions with sound business justifications, irrespective of the effect on concerted employee activity, would not be found in violation of Section 8(a) (3), which holds that it is an unfair labor practice for an employer to discriminate in employment on the basis of membership in a labor organization.[19]

The Supreme Court also evaluated the expected future benefit derived from the antiunion activity, such as discouraging collective employee activities. The Supreme Court considered this, but suggested instead that a complete liquidation of business, even though it was done for antiunion reasons, would not generate future benefits for the firm. They retreated from this statement by indicating that the expected future benefit not be in the same line of business. They stated:

> If the persons exercising control over a plant that is being closed for antiunion reasons (1) have an interest in another business, whether or not affiliated with or engaged in the same line of commercial activity as the closed plant, of sufficient substantiality to give promise of their reaping a benefit from the discouragement of unionization in that business; (2) act to close their plant with the purpose of producing such a result; and (3) occupy a relationship

to the other business which makes it realistically forseeable that its employees will fear that such business will also be closed down if they persist in organizational activities, we think that an unfair labor practice has been made out.[20]

National Labor Relations Board v. The William J. Burns International Detective Agency (346 F.2d 897) (1965)

The International Guards Union of America was certified as the collective bargaining agent for the Burns Detective Agency, guard employees in the metropolitan Omaha area. A meeting was arranged between the local Burns' manager and the union to begin negotiations. However, before this meeting took place, all but one of the establishments to which Burns provided services in the Omaha area notified Burns that they were going to cancel their service contracts with them. Burns then cancelled their service contract with the only establishment that continued to demand their services.

The manager of Burns wrote a letter to the union indicating that a negotiating session would not be necessary since Burns would not have any contracts in the Omaha area. The union filed charges against Burns alleging failure to bargain with the union as the exclusive bargaining agent. Further, it was alleged that the mere refusal to consult with the union about the termination of services is a violation of Section 8(a) (5), which defines employment conditions that require bargaining.

The Court of Appeals for the Eighth Circuit distinguished this case from *Fibreboard,* arguing that Burns had completely discontinued its operation in Omaha.

Unlike the Fibreboard situation, Burns is not continuing the same work at the same plant under similar conditions of employment. No form of contracting out or subcontracting is here involved. Burns for valid economic reasons has withdrawn completely from providing any services in the Omaha area.[21]

This case raises several intriguing questions. First, there is the juxtapositioning of the election victory by the union with the Agency's termination of its one remaining contract, thereby completely ending service in that market. Was there an antiunion animus? Second, how much can be expected of a firm when its services are no longer being demanded? It would not be able to service this market from a different location, which would be possible if this was a manufacturing facility. Third, is the expected benefit to an unfair labor practice restricted to that market of operation? Might different interpretations be necessary for manufacturing facilities as opposed to service establishments? Finally, no agreement had ever been negotiated. What was the expected return from notification and negotiation?

In terms of the labor law at the time, the only issue on which this case should have been decided was the antiunion animus. There was no substitution of employees, so *Fibreboard* would not apply. Neither would *Adams Dairy*. If it was judged that there was antiunion animus, then it must be determined whether withdrawing from this market was a partial or complete closure. Technically, Burns was closing down one part of its operation. But Burns was completely leaving this market. However, if one wants to use expected benefit in defining the status as partial or total, the answer probably is that unionization attempts could have been forestalled at other locations. Thus, it would seem that it should have been considered a partial closure, and therefore an unfair labor practice.

National Labor Relations Board v. Royal Plating and Polishing Company
(350 F.2d 191) (1965)

The Royal Plating and Polishing Company had two plants located within one block of each other. The two plants comprised a single bargaining unit. The production and maintenance workers were represented by the Metal Polishers, Buffers, Platers and Helpers International Union. A bargaining relationship had existed for 17 years, although the union had only been certified as the exclusive agent for the last 3 years. There had been little labor trouble between the union and company.

The union and company had just reached a new agreement. The Company, however, also was negotiating with the local housing authority since the property on which the plant was located was designated for redevelopment. Prior to signing the new contract with the union, the company had given the housing authority an option to purchase the plant. The housing authority exercised the option and the company closed the plant one month after the new agreement with the union had been signed.

The union charged that the company violated Sections 8(a) (5) and (1) of the National Labor Relations Act by unilaterally closing the plant. Section 8(a) (1) defines employer interference in union activities as an unfair labor practice.[22] In considering this case, the United States Court of Appeals for the Third Circuit stressed the fact that the land on which the plant was located had been designated for redevelopment by a public body. Thus, "there was no room for union negotiation in these circumstances. The union could only attempt to persuade (the owner) to move his operation to another location."[23] Also, since the decision involved a major change in the economic direction of the company, the employer did not have a duty to bargain with the union concerning the decision to shut down.

The Appeals Court did raise an important issue for effects bargaining:

> However, under the circumstances such as those presented by the case at bar an employer is still under obligation to notify the union of its intentions so that the union may be given an opportunity to bargain over the rights of the employees whose employment status will be altered by the managerial decision.[24]

This was followed by a statement that had even greater significance:

> There can be no doubt that the Company, by withholding information of its intention to terminate the Bleeker Street operations, deterred the Union from bargaining over the effect of the shutdown on the employees.[25]

This ruling dictated that there was a mandatory duty to bargain over the effects of the closure, i.e., to negotiate such issues as severance pay, vacation pay and pensions. Moreover, the phrase, "by withholding information of its intention to terminate," could be interpreted as indicating that the Court of Appeals was requiring timely advance notice be given to the employees in order to bargain over the effects. Withholding information can occur only prior to the actual occurrence. However, this interpretation has not been adopted, nor has agreement evolved on what constitutes timely advance notice.

Ozark Trailers Incorporated and International Union, Allied Industrial Workers of America, Local No. 770, AFL-CIO
(161 NLRB No. 48) (1966) (63 LRRM 1264)

The National Labor Relations Board decided this case in 1966. Ozark Trailers Incorporated was one division of a multiplant operation, although all three operations had different names. In March 1963, the Allied Industrial Workers union was certified as the bargaining agent, and in April 1963, the union and Ozark Trailers executed their first collective bargaining contract, a one-year agreement.

The following January, the board of directors of Ozark Trailers decided to close the plant for economic reasons. They claimed that low productivity, poor workmanship and an inefficiently designed facility were the reasons for the closure. No notice of closure was given to the union; in fact, the union representative was told that the layoff was temporary. The plant was closed prior to the end of the contract.

The National Labor Relations Board determined that there was a duty to bargain over the decision. Its decision was based on four separate considerations. They were:

1. Decisions important to management are likely to be important to employees.

2. The economic reasons for closing were particularly suited to resolution through collective bargaining.

3. The duty to bargain only requires that full and frank discussions of the topic be held, not that an agreement be reached by the parties.

4. Bargaining limited to the effects is not likely to be meaningful when there is no possibility of reversing the decision.

In making the argument concerning the importance of the decision to both management and employees, the Board drew the parallel between physical capital and human capital. Specifically, the Board wrote:

> For, just as the employer has invested capital in the business, so the employee has invested years of his working life, accumulating seniority, accruing pension rights, and developing skills that may or may not be salable to another employer. And, just as the employer's interest in the protection of his capital

investment is entitled to consideration in our interpretation of the Act, so too is the employee's interest in the protection of his livelihood.[26]

The second consideration drew heavily from the *Fibreboard* decision, in which the majority opinion stressed the fact that issues involving labor costs were particularly suited to resolution through the collective bargaining process. Furthermore, they pointed out that there were strong similarities between subcontracting and the partial closure, therefore rendering the latter amenable to resolution through collective bargaining.

In developing the argument pertaining to the duty to bargain, but not necessarily the duty to agree, the Board rejected the argument that this would impede management decisionmaking. The basic purposes of the National Labor Relations Act would be furthered by requiring bargaining, and since the partial closure is a relatively infrequent event, the cost to society of requiring bargaining would not be unreasonable.

The final consideration is based on the relationship between decision bargaining and effects bargaining. What is the source of bargaining power for the union when bargaining over the effects? Since it is after the fact, there is only the goodwill of the employer to rely on to generate a fair outcome. When there is a duty to bargain over the decision, potentially there is greater bargaining power because the enterprise is still an active concern. Tradeoffs can be made in the process of arriving at a decision that is mutually beneficial.

International Union, United Automobile, Aerospace and Agricultural Implement Workers of America, UAW and its Local 864, v. National Labor Relations Board
(470 F.2d 422) (1972)

General Motors (GM) owned and operated a facility in which retail trucks were sold and serviced. The employees at this facility were represented by the United Auto Workers (UAW) and had been covered by a collective bargaining agreement for four years before GM began negotiations to sell the outlet to an independent operator.

The UAW requested that they be kept informed of the potential transfer and also that GM and the UAW bargain over the decision before it was made. GM asserted there was no reason to discuss the decision until after it was made. The UAW filed suit. Subsequently, GM completed the transaction with the independent dealer. Several days later the independent dealer advised the current employees that no jobs would be available for any of them. GM officials then began discussing the effects of the sale and offered assistance in securing employment in other GM facilities.

In a marked reversal from its earlier decisions, the National Labor Relations Board ruled that the transfer was a "sale of the business." Therefore bargaining was not required under Section 8(a) (5) because this decision was at the "core of entrepreneurial control." The UAW countered that the action was a case of "contracting out" because GM maintained substantial control and essentially retained its position in the market.

The Circuit Court of Appeals sided with GM's assertion that this sale was part of a national strategy to get out of the business of running dealerships. Therefore, GM was under no obligation to bargain over the decision.

This decision was not unanimous. Judge Bazelon dissented on the grounds that there had been inadequate consideration of the employees' interest in bargaining and an overestimation of the employer's interest in not bargaining. Specifically, he wrote:

> The employer's duty to bargain may cost him time and it may threaten the confidentiality of his negotiations; these problems exist whether he is negotiating a subcontract, a sale or a franchise. But these costs can hardly be said to increase because

"title" passes, because day-to-day management
changes hands, because he used the words "buyer"
and "seller"; or even necessarily because capital is
withdrawn by the employer and invested by the
"buyer."[27]

The issue may not have been defined correctly from the
start. There had not been a change in the business. The
business operation still was engaged in the same services. The
only change had been in the financial arrangement. There
had been a substantial change in the scope of General
Motors; they were no longer in the dealership business. Conversely, they did not totally extricate themselves from this
line of business.

Brockway Motor Trucks,
Division of Mack Trucks, Inc.
v. National Labor Relations Board
(582 F.2d 720) (1978)

The United States Court of Appeals for the Third Circuit
decided this case in 1978. According to the record, Brockway
operated a number of truck manufacturing plants that also
served as sales facilities. Employees at the plant, who were
represented by the International Association of Machinists
and Aerospace Workers, were covered by a collective
bargaining agreement. After a three-year contract expired,
negotiations ensued for about nine months prior to the union
calling a strike. After two months of the strike, management
unilaterally decided to close the struck plant. Management
did not consult the union about the decision nor did it provide any advance notice of the closing.

The union brought suit arguing that management had
violated Sections 8(a) (1) and (5) of the National Labor Relations Act. Management stipulated that closing the facility
was based on "economic considerations" and was not the
result of antiunion animus. The economic considerations
necessitating closure were not specified, however.

The Board ruled that Brockway's action violated Section 8(a) (5) because when an action directly affects the conditions of employment, there is a duty to bargain irrespective of the assertion that the requirement significantly restricts the employer's ability to run the business. Moreover, the Board ruled that there is only a duty to bargain, not necessarily a duty to reach an agreement.

The Court of Appeals first of all stressed the need to specify the economic considerations leading to the decision to close one plant or change the direction of the business. In recounting previous cases in which economic considerations had been at issue and the finding had been that there was no duty to bargain, it noted that economic considerations were major ones such as being necessary to remain in business or the firm having lost considerable sums of money.

Both parties advanced *per se* rules. Brockway asserted that "when a partial closing is predicated on 'economic consideration,' whatever they may be, there can be no duty to bargain about it."[28] The Board's rule was "that an employer has a duty to bargain about a decision to close one of its facilities, for such an action intimately affects the interests of the employees and is the sort of subject that the NLRA was designed to reach."[29] The Court of Appeals rejected both *per se* approaches and attempted to fashion an alternative.

They started with the premise that the aims of collective bargaining would be furthered by requiring negotiations between an employer and the union before irrevocably closing a plant. They also added that closing a plant was likely to lead to the termination of employment and therefore it might be called a "condition of employment." Thus, the initial presumption was that "a partial closing is a mandatory subject of bargaining."[30]

However, because the Court had rejected both *per se* rules, additional analysis was necessary after the initial presumption. First, the Appeals Court stated that the interest of the employees in bargaining must be considered since, in most circumstances, it is hard to imagine that workers would not have a strong interest in trying to change a decision that affected their employment.

The next element to be considered is the likelihood that the decision could be altered through the bargaining process. The Court recognized that there are certain areas in which the union has greater or lesser expertise and control. The area of labor costs is one area in which labor has more control. Thus, there is a positive likelihood that bargaining can be successful. Furthermore, as in *Fibreboard,* the Appeals Court cited that considerable bargaining had taken place over plant closure.

The final element to consider is the employer's countervailing interest in not bargaining. To presume that all economic considerations outweigh the employee's interest is as inappropriate as arguing that management's interest could never be so great as to eliminate the duty to bargain over the decision. The Court stated that it could not use the balancing test in this case because Brockway did not specify the nature of the economic considerations.[31]

First National Maintenance Corporation v. National Labor Relations Board
(101 S. Ct. 2573) (1981)

The most recent ruling of the United States Supreme Court on the plant closure issue was its decision in *First National Maintenance.* The facts of this case are as follows. The company provided housekeeping, cleaning, maintenance and related services for commercial customers in the New York City area. In return for the maintenance services, the company was reimbursed for its labor costs and also received a set management fee. Personnel were hired separately for each contract (location) and employees were not transferred among locations.

In March 1977 a certification election was conducted among the employees at this location, and the National

Union of Hospital and Health Care Employees was certified as the bargaining agent. First National Maintenance Corporation (FNM) was experiencing difficulties with a purchaser of its services at this time due to disagreement over the management fee. In July the union wrote FNM of its desire to begin negotiations. FNM never responded. Later in July, FNM notified the purchaser of its maintenance services that it was cancelling the agreement unless the management fee was increased. The purchaser would not increase the fee, the agreement was cancelled and the employees were given three days notice that they were being discharged.

The union filed an unfair labor practice charge against FNM charging that FNM interfered in the activities of the union, Section 8(a) (1), and refused to bargain with the elected representatives of the union, Section 8(a) (5). Both the Administrative Law Judge and the National Labor Relations Board adopted the position that FNM had failed to satisfy its duty to bargain about the decision to terminate or about the effects. The Court of Appeals adopted the position of the Board, but put forth a different line of reasoning. Following *Brockway,* they indicated that no *per se* rule was appropriate under the law. Rather, there was a presumption in favor of mandatory bargaining over the decision, with that position being rebuttable if the purposes of Section 8(d) would not be furthered. Examples of such circumstances might include:

1. Bargaining would be futile.

2. The decision to close was due to emergency financial circumstances.

3. Firms in that industry customarily had not bargained over such decisions, as demonstrated by their absence from collective bargaining contracts.

The Supreme Court's majority decision, which was written by Justice Blackmun, did not adopt the rebuttable presumption rule developed by the Court of Appeals. Instead, it developed its own balancing test.

> In view of an employer's need for unencumbered decisionmaking, bargaining over management decisions that have a substantial impact on the continued availability of employment should be required only if the benefit, for labor-management relations and the collective bargaining process, outweighs the burden placed on the conduct of business.[32]

The Supreme Court, on the basis of its balancing test, determined that the employer's need to operate freely outweighed the incremental benefits that might arise from permitting the union to participate in the decision. Therefore, when a business is shut down for purely economic reasons, there is no mandatory duty to bargain over the decision under Section 8(d). If the shutdown is due to an anti-union animus, the duty to bargain is protected under Section 8(a) (3), which prohibits discrimination on the basis of union membership.

The Supreme Court took great pains to limit the generalizability of the holding. First, they wrote: "In this opinion we of course intimate no view as to other types of management decisions, such as plant relocations, sales, other kinds of subcontracting, automation, etc., which are to be considered on their own particular facts."[33] Second, the Court noted that the union had no control over the size of the management fee, which was the reason for closing. Thus, bargaining would not have been a factor in changing management's mind. Third, the Court pointed out that the management fee had been an issue prior to the selection of the union as the bargaining representative.

Because of the caveats given by the Court, it must be questioned whether they established a *per se* rule for shutdowns of operations based on economic reasons. It appears that the Court felt it established a *per se* rule because it expounded on the difficulties of case-by-case adjudication such as would be necessary under the rebuttable presumption rule. First, the employer never totally knows if his shutdown requires bargaining or not. Second, if the employer bargains and does not reach an agreement, he does not know with certainty whether he has met the requirements for good faith bargaining. Third, if the employer does not bargain, feeling that the purposes of the Section 8(d) would not be advanced, and is incorrect, the potential cost of that decision could be onerous due to the requirement of paying wages back to the day of the decision.

The Supreme Court raised the most pertinent issue. What is the real purpose of requiring bargaining over the decision to close? Is the purpose to compel discussion of the closure? Is it to forestall closure or is it to provide information? The Court adopted the positions that (a) the union will seek to halt the shutdown, (b) bargaining will occur voluntarily—initiated by management—if labor costs are an important consideration, and (c) requiring bargaining will not improve the flow of information.

The counter position is that information will not be made available without mandatory bargaining. Information is needed to determine (a) the reason for the shutdown and (b) what changes will be necessary to continue operations if the reason for shutting down is amenable to bargaining. Once that information is available, the union can make the decision whether it should pursue bargaining. This issue is addressed at greater depth in the next chapter.

Negotiations in the formal contract also were used as evidence. Whereas the majority in *Fibreboard* drew upon current practice in negotiated contracts to find a duty to bargain over subcontracting, the majority in *First National Maintenance* cited current practices to find no duty to bargain over the decision to close. Specifically, they wrote: "We note that provisions giving unions a right to participate in the decisionmaking process concerning alteration of the scope of an enterprise appear to be relatively rare. Provisions concerning notice and 'effects' bargaining are more prevalent."[34]

In conclusion, due to the facts of this case, the Supreme Court probably only could rule that there was no duty to bargain over the decision. It is questionable, however, whether this case should serve as a significant precedent for future decisions. It is severely limited due to the facts of the case.

Los Angeles Marine Hardware Company v. National Labor Relations Board
(602 F. 2d 1302) (1979)

A significant recent development in labor law concerns the relocation of work during the course of the collective bargaining agreement. The position that has been taken by the National Labor Relations Board, which has been upheld by the United States Court of Appeals, is that the relocation of work, even if it is for economic reasons, while the contract is in force, violates Sections 8(a) (1) and (5) and Section (d) of the National Labor Relations Act. Although several cases have helped to develop this rule, the two principal cases are *Los Angeles Marine* and *Milwaukee Spring* which are discussed below.

Mission Marine Associates was a holding company for two divisions, Los Angeles Marine Hardware Company and California Marine Hardware Company. Cal Marine was an inactive shell prior to March 1977 whereas LA Marine was an active division. LA Marine had an established bargaining relationship with the Chauffeurs, Sales Drivers, Warehousemen and Helpers Union dating back to 1956.

LA Marine was facing potential operating deficits that in part were due to the high union wages it was paying. The company tried to obtain relief from the union during the 1975 round of negotiations, but was unsuccessful. The company met with the union in 1977, indicated it was planning to relocate and proposed a new contract for the relocation. The union refused to discuss the matter, given the existing contract. The company proceeded with the relocation, terminated the union workers and activated Cal Marine.

For purposes of establishing whether an unfair labor practice had been committed, it was determined that LA Marine and Cal Marine were the same employer. Cal Marine was simply continuing the operations of LA Marine and, therefore, the relocation, firing of union workers and establishing a new pay schedule all constituted mid-term repudiations of the contract. LA Marine countered that the collective bargaining agreement only covered work done at the old location.

The two principal legal points made by the Appeals Court were:

1. An employer cannot alter mandatory contractual terms while a contract is in effect without the agreement of the union.

2. An employer is not relieved of its duty to recognize the union by relocating when the relocation is an unfair labor practice.

The results potentially could generate some interesting twists. The unfair labor practice arose because the terms and conditions of the collective bargaining agreement were not applied to the new employees at the new location—wages had been changed unilaterally. What if the company had simply relocated from LA Marine to Cal Marine and had not lowered wages? Would this have been a strict instance of relocation and therefore not subject to bargaining? The firm could have used this tactic and then subsequently sought decertification and reduced the wage costs at the new location, say one year later. The reason for the relocation could simply have been a more efficient structure or the potential for a more efficient operation.

According to one writer, "good faith bargaining under Section 8(a) (5) requires not only that the parties abide by the provisions of the collective bargaining agreement, but that neither party will undermine, circumvent, or avoid the provisions of the agreement." (Bosanac 1983) Conversely, another writer indicated that "An employer that is not specifically prohibited by an agreement from relocating bargaining unit work during the term of the agreement retains the right, after bargaining, to relocate that work during the term of the agreement if the relocation is taken in response to a need to reduce high labor costs." (Klaper 1983)

It is obvious that there is considerable disagreement about the extent of this ruling. It also brings out the fragile demarcation that exists between unfair labor practice cases and justifiable actions. Specifically, according to the Board's ruling, the unfair labor practice did not arise from relocating the work, it was due to reducing wages. Had the company argued that the new work relocation was more efficient, and had it maintained the collective bargaining agreement, the employer's actions most likely would not have been found to be an unfair labor practice.[35]

Milwaukee Spring Division of Illinois Coil Spring Company and United Automobile Workers (UAW) and its Local 547
(265 NLRB No. 28, 111 LRRM 1486) (1982)

This case was decided by the National Labor Relations Board in 1982. The Board applied the theory developed in *Los Angeles Marine* to decide this case.

The facts of this case were as follows. The parent company, Illinois Coil Spring Company, had a union facility in Milwaukee and a nonunion facility in McHenry, Illinois. While a contract was in effect at the Milwaukee facility, the company asked the union to forego a wage increase and to grant other contract concessions, partially because some business had been lost. The company then proposed to relocate the assembly operations from Milwaukee to McHenry, where wage payments were considerably lower. The union refused to grant the concessions, but it did indicate that it was willing to continue discussions. The company proceeded with the plans to relocate the work to the McHenry facility.

The union charged that the decision to relocate work during the course of the contract constituted a mid-term repudiation of the collective bargaining contract. The relocation was due solely to the desire to go from the higher labor costs at the union facility to the lower labor costs at the nonunion facility.

The company asserted that because it had engaged in decision bargaining, and because it had offered to engage in effects bargaining, it could relocate the work. Furthermore this was possible because the collective bargaining agreement had no express prohibition against relocation.

The Board ruled that the company's relocation of work during the contract violated Section 8(d) because the union had not waived its right to object to the move, even though it had bargained over it, and the collective bargaining contract also did not contain language indicating the union had un-equivocally waived its right to object to the relocation. Specifically, the Board wrote:

> The Board has held that Section 8(d) forbids altera-tion by an employer of the terms and conditions of employment embodied in a collective bargaining agreement during the term of the agreement without the consent of the union, even though the employer may have previously offered to bargain with the union about the change and the union has refused.[36]

Both the company and the union were bound by the terms of the collective bargaining contract while it was in force.

In some respects, the thrust of the decision is counter-productive. Consider the following scenario. A collective bargaining contract is in force. The firm begins to experience financial difficulty. It approaches the union for some assistance in making it through the period of difficulty. However, no agreement is reached with the union to alter mandatory terms. The firm has four choices.

1. The company can close the operation and there is no violation of Section 8(d).

2. The company can continue operating at the facility until the financial difficulties become so severe that it has no choice but to close the facility. There is no violation of Section 8(d).

3. The company can operate the facility until the contract expires, at which time it proposes Draconian terms. If no agreement is reached, it can relocate the work without violating Section 8(d).

4. The company can relocate the work in an attempt to obtain financial relief and incur a violation of Section 8(d).

Loss of markets or other financial difficulties do not necessarily occur on the same cycle as the collective bargaining contract. As the options above indicate, without a mechanism for mid-term flexibility, all or nothing solutions will be used. It is somewhat incongruous that closure is a "legal" solution whereas relocation while a contract is in effect is not, even though both can generate the same impact on the workers at the site.[37]

Although an appeal had been filed with the Seventh Circuit Court of Appeals, the National Labor Relation Board requested that *Milwaukee Spring I* be remanded to the Board. In July 1983, the Court of Appeals relinquished jurisdiction; oral arguments were presented in September 1983 and the Board reversed its decision January 1984 in *Milwaukee Spring II* (268 NLRB No. 87).

In reversing its decision, the NLRB ruled that the firm did not violate Section 8(a) of the National Labor Relations Act because the contract did not expressly cover the condition—relocating work from one facility to another. Since there was no contract provision under which the union had to agree to a change, Milwaukee Spring's obligation simply was to bargain in good faith to impasse over moving work before instituting the change.

The Board adopted the logic presented in *Los Angeles Marine*, but to the advantage of the employer. The Board agreed that the contract was still in force at the Milwaukee facility and there had been no change in terms and conditions at that facility. Had any workers been employed at the Milwaukee location, they would have been entitled to the contractually agreed on wages.

This writer's reading of the opinion suggests that an unintended precedent may have been set. It appears that the

Board considered relocation of work a mandatory topic of bargaining. Specifically, the Board wrote: "If the employment conditions the employer seeks to change are not 'contained in' the contract, however, the employer's obligation remains the general one of bargaining in good faith to impasse over the subject before instituting the proposed change." Prior to this ruling, relocation was not necessarily considered a term or condition of employment. The wording in this context implies that it is.

Although the NLRB has ruled that a firm can relocate its work, this question is still not resolved. Specifically, there now is a "split in the circuits." *Los Angeles Marine* also still serves as a precedent. Depending on which case a court relies on—*Los Angeles Marine* or *Milwaukee Spring II*—the outcome could be quite different, with vastly different cost implications for firms.

Summary and Conclusions

The summation of the 12 cases, provided in table 3.1, indicates several disturbing features of the decisions. They are (a) the concern with process and not outcomes, (b) the unspecified nature of economic considerations, (c) the treatment of antiunion animus, (d) the sharp distinction between relocation and plant closure, and (e) effects bargaining.

The concern with process and not outcomes is very evident in the *Fibreboard* and *Adams Dairy* cases. What is the difference in the outcomes between replacing drivers-salesmen with independent contractors to distribute and market products, and subcontracting out maintenance activities that had been performed by employees? In both instances, employees were replaced with nonemployees. Both activities were designed to reduce the costs of a particular operation. The products produced did not change nor did the firms change their lines of business. They did not change their attachment to a particular market. They changed an activity. Although *Adams Dairy* did engage in some disinvestment of capital because it no longer needed to own a fleet of trucks, it is an overstatement to say that it was a major change in the operation of business.

Conversely, suppose *Adams Dairy* had not been able to reduce its labor costs associated with the delivery of its product and had gone out of business as a result. That would not have been a satisfactory solution, either. Numerous employees would have lost their jobs. Thus, the distinction between *Fibreboard* and *Adams Dairy* is unclear, and therefore, the determination whether there is a duty to bargain over the decision on the basis of terminology of the process.

In this regard, consider the *UAW-GM* dealership case. There was no change in the actual business, the dealership. Ownership of it had changed by means of a sale. Although GM was changing the nature of its business, there was no change in the product/service nor probably in the skills of the individuals necessary to produce the product/service. However, because it was a sale, the NLRB considered it a totally different situation, even though the impact on the employees was the same as closure.

Economic considerations are evident in all of these cases. Examples could include unsatisfactory profits, loss of market share, high labor costs, poor workmanship and low productivity, and managerial difficulties with clients/suppliers. All of these are economic difficulties and considerations. The key difference is that some issues are more likely to be resolved through collective bargaining, whereas in other situations the economic considerations are likely to be beyond the scope of the bargaining relationship.

Consider *Los Angeles Marine* and *Milwaukee Spring I* in this light. The economic difficulty was high labor costs in the former, and high labor costs and a lost subcontract in the lat-

Table 3.1
Summary of Major Decisions on Subcontracting and Partial Closure Cases

Case	Major issue	Resolution	Significant precedent (comments)
Fibreboard (1964)	Is there a duty to bargain over subcontracting?	Duty to bargain when employees are substituted and there is no capital investment.	Subcontracting, as defined in this case, is a term and condition of employment.
Adams Dairy (1963)	Is there a duty to bargain over a change in service, using independent contractors instead of employees?	No duty to bargain over the decision because change was made for legitimate business reasons.	(Fine line distinction between subcontracting and changing one's distribution system.)
Darlington (1965)	Is closing a plant because of union organization an unfair labor practice?	Complete freedom to close entire business even if it is due to antiunion animus.	Established demarcation between complete closure and partial closure.
Burns Detective (1965)	Is there a duty to bargain over the decision to close one operation of a multiplant operation?	No duty to bargain over the discontinuance of an operation.	(The issue of antiunion animus was not addressed appropriately in this case.)
Royal Plating (1965)	Is there a duty to bargain over the decision to close one plant of a multiplant operation?	No duty to bargain over the decision to make a major change in the economic direction of the company.	The effects of closure fall within the meaning of terms and conditions of employment. Thus, there is a mandatory duty to bargain over the effects.
Ozark Trailers (1966)	Is there a duty to bargain over the decision to close one plant of a multiplant operation when closure is due to economic considerations?	There is a duty to bargain over the decision when the economic considerations are amenable to bargaining, such as poor workmanship and low productivity.	(This decision stressed the importance of the employees' human capital investment in the firm.)

Case	Issue	Holding	Comment
UAW (1972)	Is there a duty to bargain over the decision to convert a self-owned and operated outlet into an independently owned franchise?	No duty to bargain because the action constituted the sale of a business which is at the core of entrepreneurial control.	(Although ownership changed, there was no real change in the business. Marked change in NLRB position.)
Brockway (1979)	Is there a duty to bargain over the partial closure of an operation when the decision to close is for unspecified economic considerations?	No *per se* rule is acceptable. Determination of duty depends on the interest in bargaining and probability of success.	The court developed a three part test of when there is a duty to bargain over the decision.
First National Maintenance (1981)	Is there a duty to bargain over the cessation of a service contract when it is one of several contracts?	No duty to bargain because the benefits of bargaining would not outweigh the costs imposed on the employer.	The precedent is limited by the facts of the case. (Very poor case to serve as a precedent.)
Los Angeles Marine (1979)	Can company transfer work, which results in closure, while a contract is in force without the union's acquiescence?	Employer cannot alter mandatory contractual terms while a contract is in effect without the agreement of the union.	Creates strong distinction between closure and relocation.
Milwaukee Spring I (1982)	Does relocation of work from union facility to nonunion facility represent mid-term contract repudiation?	Relocation of work during contract violates Section 8(d) because union had not waived rights.	Increases distinction between closure and relocation. (Creates serious dilemma for firms in financial difficulties.)
Milwaukee Spring II (1984)	Does relocation of work from union facility to nonunion facility represent mid-term contract repudiation?	Relocation of work during contract does not violate Section 8(d) unless there is a provision in the contract prohibiting relocation of work.	Relocation is a mandatory topic of bargaining. (Creates split in the circuits with *Los Angeles Marine*.)

ter. The higher labor costs also were coupled, though, with having alternate facilities available. Presumably, it would have been possible in both cases to begin bidding projects from the alternate plant. As projects were completed at the current facility, those workers could be phased out, and the plant eventually closed. Instead, at least in the latter case, they attempted to negotiate. What could have facilitated those negotiations so that they would have resulted in satisfactory outcomes for both management and labor? The ruling in *Milwaukee Spring II* comes closer to this position by implicitly holding that relocation is a mandatory topic of bargaining.

The treatment of antinuion animus also is problematic throughout these cases. Darlington closed to avoid having to negotiate a contract with the duly elected representatives of the workers. Burns Detective Agency closed shortly after a representation victory. Ozark Trailers closed one year after a representation election was won by the union. First National Maintenance decided to discontinue the particular operations shortly after the representation election was won by the union. Only in *Darlington* were there no mitigating circumstances, however. The juxtapositioning of certification and closure has clouded (a) whether there is a duty to bargain, (b) whether the reason for closure is amenable to resolution through collective bargaining, and (c) whether antiunion animus is present in these cases.

Are there differences in the nature of markets and goods and services produced that should impact on the determination of antiunion animus? For example, in *Darlington* the Supreme Court's ruling was partially premised on the rationalization that there must be some potential benefit for the firm from unfair labor practices in order for there to be a judgment of antiunion animus. Thus, complete closure would generate no future benefits because the owner would not be in business to take advantage of them.

Partial closure of a manufacturing facility would generate these benefits because (a) the company still could serve the market with goods produced at the other facility and (b) the action would have a chilling effect on union organizing activities at the other plants.

Would partial closure of a service operation arising from antiunion animus generate these same benefits? For a firm providing services, the market area is limited geographically. It may not be possible to provide the same services from a geographically separate location. Thus, the closure of a service establishment is tantamount to complete closure; it is a total withdrawal from a market. However, the diffusion of the information and the benefit derived from an unfair labor practice are not restricted in the same way. The timing of the representation election victory and the closure of the Omaha operation in *Burns Detective* could have sent a clear signal to other establishments, if they were not already organized, that selection of a representative could result in closure.

Another area of concern is the sharp distinction that has arisen between relocation and plant closure. The outcomes for the employees, again, are the same—loss of employment. However, in the former case it might be suggested that the economic considerations in the decision to relocate are not quite as severe as they are in the closure decision. The judicial interpretations encourage the firms to take the more drastic step, closing the facility. As spelled out in *Milwaukee Spring I,* the firm could escape the unfair labor practice charge by closing the plant outright. However, the firm could not relocate the work because it is an unfair labor practice.

Milwaukee Spring II maintains the distinction between relocation and closure, and some of the logic is questionable. But the broad interpretation, which mandates bargaining over relocation but permits relocation during the contract if the bargainers reach impasse, is more consistent with maintaining profitable operations and employment.

The final issue is effects bargaining. There seems to be no disagreement that bargaining over the effects of closure is a mandatory topic of bargaining under Section 8(a) (5). The closing bargain is the last resort position. "Effects bargaining usually involves rights of employees that arise as a result of closing, such as severance pay, pensions, other accrued benefits, grievances and possible reemployment in other parts of an employer's enterprise." (Heinsz 1981)

Whether actual bargaining can take place when there is only a duty to bargain over the effects must be questioned. The Appeals Court in *Royal Plating and Polishing* wrote:

> There can be no doubt that the Company, by withholding information of its intention to terminate the Bleeker Street operations, deterred the Union from bargaining over the effect of the shutdown on the employees.[38]

The Board in *Ozark Trailers* doubted the meaningfulness of bargaining over the effects when there is no possibility of reversing the decision.

If effects bargaining could be combined with decision bargaining, a number of the concerns expressed above could be alleviated. First, notice would be given so the plant would still be in operation. Second, tradeoffs could be made between the duties to bargain. For example, the union could waive future effects bargaining, with its associated cost, in return for a commitment to keep the plant operating. On the other hand, the union could seek a more attractive closing bargain by waiving the duty to bargain over the decision to close.

In conclusion, the judicial interpretations of the duty to bargain over the decision to shut down a plant are problematic. The decisions reviewed have demonstrated (a) the concern with process and not outcome , (b) the unspecified nature or narrow interpretation of economic considerations, (c) the treatment of antiunion animus, (d) the sharp distinction between relocation and plant closure, and (e) effects bargaining.

The uncertainties associated with case-by-case adjudication have prompted some students of these issue to propose alternatives, such as *per se* rules which would define more clearly when there is a duty to bargain over the decision to close. These *per se* rules, which would require a legislative amendment to the National Labor Relations Act or enunciation by the United States Supreme Court, are presented and evaluated in the next chapter.

NOTES

1. The administrative procedure requires that charges of unfair labor practices be filed with the National Labor Relations Board. The regional staff of the NLRB investigates the charges and attempts to promote a settlement. If the Regional Director files a complaint, a hearing is held before an Administrative Law Judge (ALJ).

If a party disagrees with the finding by the ALJ, it can appeal to the NLRB in Washington. That appeal is heard by a team composed of three of the five appointed members of the National Labor Relations Board. Appeals to the NLRB's decision are filed with the United States Circuit Court of Appeals. Finally, the United States Supreme Court may agree to hear an appeal of the decision of the circuit court.

2. *Fibreboard Paper Products Corporation v. National Labor Relations Board,* 85 S. Ct. 398 (1964).

3. *National Labor Relations Board v. Royal Plating and Polishing Company,* 350 F. 2d 191 (1965).

4. *Ozark Trailers Incorporated and International Union, Allied Industrial Workers of America,* 161 NLRB No. 48 (1966).

5. 161 NLRB No. 48.

6. *Textile Workers Union of America v. Darlington Manufacturing Company, et al., and National Labor Relations Board v. Darlington Manufacturing Company, et al.,* 85 S. Ct. 994 (1965).

7. *First National Maintenance Corporation v. National Labor Relations Board,* 101 S. Ct. 2573 (1981).

8. National Labor Relations Act, Section 8(d).

9. 101 S. Ct. 2573 (1981).

10. 101 S. Ct. 2573, 2585.

11. 101 S. Ct. 2573, 2585.

12. *National Labor Relations Board v. Wooster Division of Borg-Warner Corporation,* 78 S. Ct. 718, 723 (1958).

13. 85 S. Ct. 398, 402 (1964).

14. 85 S. Ct. 398, 405 (1964).

15. 85 S. Ct. 398, 409, 410 (1964).

16. *National Labor Relations Board v. Adams Dairy, Inc.,* 322 F.2d 553, 557 (1963).

17. 322 F.2d 553, 562 (1963).

18. *Textile Workers Union of America v. Darlington Manufacturing Company et al., and National Labor Relations Board v. Darlington Manufacturing Company et al.,* 85 S. Ct. 994, 998 (1965).

19. The Court asked the question of whether there is a symmetrical obligation or lack of one between employees and employer. They quoted from the Court of Appeals the following statement: The Act "does not compel a person to become or remain an employee. It does not compel one to become or remain an employer. Either may withdraw from that status with immunity, so long as the obligations of any employment contract have been met." (*Darlington Manufacturing Company v. Textile Workers Union of America,* 384 F.2d 682, 685 (1963)).

20. 85 S. Ct. 994, 1002 (1965).

21. *National Labor Relations Board v. The William J. Burns International Detective Agency,* 346 F.2d 897, 903 (1965).

22. This section became an issue because closure could be seen as violating free speech protections.

23. 350 F.2d 191, 195 (1965).

24. 350 F.2d 191, 196 (1965).

25. 350 F.2d 191, 196 (1965).

26. 63 LRRM 1264, 1267 (1966).

27. *International Union, United Automobile, Aerospace and Agricultural Implement Workers of America, UAW and its Local 864 v. National Labor Relations Board,* 470 F.2d 422, 428 (1972).

28. *Brockway Motor Trucks Division of Mack Trucks, Inc. v. National Labor Relations Board,* 582 F.2d 720 (1978).

29. 582 F.2d 720, 732 (1978).

30. 582 F.2d 720, 735 (1978).

31. 582 F.2d 720, 745-749 (1978).

32. 101 S. Ct. 2573, 2581 (1981).

33. 101 S. Ct. 2573, 2585 (1981).

34. 101 S. Ct. 2573, 2583 (1981).

35. Bosanac (1983) wrote: "Work transfers, *per se,* are not proscribed under the *Los Angeles Marine* theory. Only when transfers of work become the means to achieving improper ends, midcontract modification, do they become illegal." (p. 76).

36. *Milwaukee Spring Division of Illinois Coil Spring Company and United Automobile Workers (UAW) and its Local 547,* 111 LRRM 1486 (1982).

37. Two other cases that fall within this general area are: *Brown Company; Brown Company, Livingston-Graham Division; Brown Company, Tri-City Concrete Division; L-T Transport, Inc. and Kris A. Borum et al.* 243 NLRB, No. 100 (1979), 1979 CCH NLRB #16082. *Tocco Division of Park-Ohio Industries, Inc., and Auto Workers, Local 91, UAW.* (257 NLRB No. 44) (107 LRRM 1498) (1981).

38. 350 F.2d 191, 196 (1965).

Chapter 4

The Duty to Bargain
Per Se Rules

Introduction

A number of the students of labor-management relations, as well as the National Labor Relations Board and the Courts, have attempted to develop guidelines, tests or rules for determining whether and under what conditions there is a duty to bargain over the decision to close. Naturally, the determination could be made on a case-by-case basis, but that is extremely costly. As St. Antoine (1981) has written, "this has the attraction of maximizing fairness in individual situations, but it can lead to uncertainty and unpredictability."

Notions of equity have led to the rejection of the polar *per se* rules: (a) there is no duty to bargain over partial plant closures, relocations or major technological changes resulting in large scale displacement of labor; (b) there is a mandatory duty to bargain over all decisions leading to the permanent displacement or dislocation of workers from a particular employment. Furthermore, the more recent rulings on mid-term contract repudiations also are unsatisfactory because they encourage closure rather than achieving a solution that maintains employment and profitable operations.

The guidelines, tests or rules that have been suggested have several features in common. They hope to cover as many of the potential circumstances as possible without requiring bargaining in all situations. Also, they hope to be straightforward and easily interpretable so as to create the least confusion possible. The four approaches to be considered below are Schwarz's employment substitution rule, Rabin's seven point guideline, the three part test developed in Brockway and Heinsz's rule of rebuttable presumption. This chapter ends with the presentation of a new proposal addressing the determination of the duty to bargain over the decision to close.

Employment Substitution Rule

Schwarz (1970) proposed the employment substitution rule in his article, "Plant Relocation or Partial Termination-The Duty to Decision-Bargain." The rule is:

> Decision-bargaining should be required in all cases where the employer plans to substitute non-unit workers for unit workers.

It is a straightforward restatement of the decision presented in *Fibreboard Paper Products Corporation v. National Labor Relations Board,* which involved "the replacement of employees in the existing bargaining unit with those of an independent contractor to do the same work under similar conditions of employment."[1] However, whereas the above represented a definition of contracting out, Schwarz's rule also would apply to relocations.

Schwarz's approach has the desirability of being straightforward. There are no probability statements associated with it. The union would need to be consulted if employment is substituted; if not, there would be no need for consultation.

However, this rule would not require bargaining in all circumstances where a solution may be forthcoming and would require bargaining in others where perhaps there is no possibility of a solution being reached. To evaluate this, it is necessary to develop a taxonomy of closures. They can take the following forms:

1. The firm continues operations at the location, but some employees are displaced by individuals who have been contracted to perform the same duties.

2. The firm relocates its operation so that it is producing the same or similar product in a different facility and with new employees.

3. The plant closes because it is no longer competitive due to high labor costs or low productivity.

4. The plant closes or relocates because the present market for its product no longer exists.

The employment substitution rule would require decision bargaining in the first two instances, and also sometimes in the fourth circumstance. It would not apply in the third instance, which may be the critical one. According to Schmenner's (1982) analysis, high labor costs or work rules were the principal reason for closure in over one-fifth of the cases. Thus, the expectation is that negotiations possibly could save jobs and restore profitable operations in the third instance, yet decision bargaining would not be required.

Bargaining could be required when there is no possibility of a solution being reached. This rule would require bargaining when a firm relocates its operation because the present market for its product no longer exists. For instance, consider the firm that has been a supplier to a firm that has relocated. In order to stay in business, it is forced to relocate to an area in which it can negotiate new contracts. It still is in the same line of business, although it has substituted employees. Bargaining would have a very low probability of altering the decision to relocate. In this instance, effects bargaining would be more important.

Rabin's Seven Point Criteria

Rabin (1971) proposed a seven point criteria for determining when there should be and when there should not be a mandatory duty to bargain over the decision to close a plant. The seven points are as follows:

1. The impact on employees must be certain and direct.

2. The decision must not be minor or recurrent.

3. The issue must be within the expertise of both parties.

4. The decision to terminate operations must be based on factors that are not so compelling that the bargaining process could not possibly alter them.

5. An "established," not merely "technical," bargaining relationship must have been in effect prior to the decision.

6. The statutory requirement of good faith bargaining, particularly as to notice, must be interpreted flexibly so that the employers freedom to act is not unduly impeded.

7. The parties should be given wide latitude to allocate management functions by consent.

The first two points remove such decisions as new sales or marketing strategies, which may ultimately diminish employment, from mandatory bargaining. Conversely, a plant closing, a major technological change or a relocation all have certain and direct impact on employment in the short run and do not necessarily recur on a regular basis. Therefore, decision bargaining would be mandatory on these issues assuming the other criteria are met.

The third and fourth points establish that the reason for the relocation or partial closure possibly could be altered through the bargaining process in order to mandate decision bargaining. Stating that the "issue must be within the expertise of both parties" can be interpreted narrowly or expansively. The narrow interpretation would hold that only labor costs and work rules would be within the expertise of both parties. A more expansive interpretation would contend that production processes, major purchases of equipment and perhaps new markets also fall in the area of expertise of both parties. The quality of work life movement, quality circles and other manifestations of labor-management cooperation have shown that production processes and the general operation of facilities also are within the expertise of some labor organizations.

The definition of compelling factors is not sufficiently clear to forestall case-by-case adjudication. For example, is loss of a key source of a factor of production a compelling reason? Consider the case when another source becomes available, albeit at a higher price. The higher price does not permit profitable production of the product, but bargaining with the union results in labor costs being reduced so that production can be resumed with the new source of the factor, and the output can be sold at a profit. Although the compelling reason was altered through bargaining, the probability of bargaining being successful in this instance is likely to be quite low.

Restricting the duty to bargain to established bargaining relationships would accomplish two things. First, it would separate the duty to bargain controversy, Section (8) (d), from the unfair labor practices issue, Section (8) (a) (3). If a closing occurred on the heels of a union representation election, without a contract formally bargained, the issue could simply be settled on whether this was an unfair labor practice. By bringing in the duty to bargain, precedents are established about the duty to bargain even though no bargaining has ever occurred.

Second, there would be a history of bargaining between the two parties which could be built upon in developing expectations for a settlement. Several cases, the most important being *First National Maintenance Corporation v. National Labor Relations Board,* involved a situation where the union selected in the representation election never had negotiated a contract with the employer. Thus, the facts of the case did not lend themselves to making a judgment about the potential efficacy of bargaining.

One criticism raised frequently of the duty to decision bargain is that there is no incentive for the union to reach an agreement concerning the potential closure because the longer bargaining continues, the longer the plant remains in operation. Furthermore, there is the fear that breaking off negotiations, even if no progress is being made, will be judged as failure to bargain in good faith, with penalties assessed accordingly. Rabin's sixth point, by suggesting flexibility in the interpretation of good faith bargaining, hopes to encourage sincere bargaining by ensuring that the process can be ended without requiring management to reach an unfavorable bargain. However, a flexible interpretation does not necessarily reduce uncertainty or unpredictability until after sufficient experience exists to develop a reasonable expectation of the definition of flexible interpretation of good faith bargaining.

Mature bargaining relationships may specify prerogatives of both management and labor in the bargaining contract. Rabin's seventh point suggests that judicial interpretations should not overrule these prerogatives so that both partners can be reasonably certain about what issues they must negotiate and those in which management can act unilaterally without fear of being found in violation of the National Labor Relations Act.

It is very ironic that neither Schwarz's employment substitution rule nor the seven point criteria developed by Rabin would have required the First National Maintenance Corporation to negotiate with the union over the decision to close. Yet this case served as the vehicle for the most recent United States Supreme Court ruling on the duty to bargain in partial plant closures.

Three Part Test of Brockway

The majority opinion in *Brockway Motor Trucks, Division of Mack Trucks, Inc., v. National Labor Relations Board* took exception with *per se* rules that either mandate no duty to bargain or mandate a duty to bargain in all cases of plant closure. The majority opinion reflected that the basic problem is that no simple *per se* rule can adequately protect the interests of all parties in all of the factually divergent situations in which shutdowns may occur. The opinion also took exception to the argument by Brockway Motor Trucks that because the closure was due to "economic considerations," although unspecified, there was no duty to bargain.

Instead, the majority opinion fashioned a three part test to determine when bargaining should be mandated in cases of partial plant closure. The three considerations are as follows:

1. The strength of the employees' interest in altering management's decision.

2. The likelihood that bargaining would lead the employer to alter its decision.

3. Management's countervailing interest in not bargaining.

The major problem with this three part test is that the determination of the duty to bargain must be adjudicated. The firm planning to close one part of its operation would not know with certainty whether it can do so without bargaining because both the strength of the employees' interest and the countervailing interest of management cannot be evaluated a priori.

The strength of the employees' interest in altering management's decision requires two pieces of information, of which only one can be obtained through the bargaining process. First, the probability of obtaining alternate employment and at what wage elsewhere in the area must be established. Second, the concession necessary to change management's decision also must become known. If alternate employment opportunities are available at essentially the same wage rate, employees may have only a weak interest in changing the decision to close. Conversely, if the next best employment alternative, the opportunity wage, is considerably less than that received from the current employer, the interest in altering management's decision may be quite strong. It might be suggested that the strength of interest is directly proportional to the divergence between the current wage and the opportunity wage. But the union would not attempt to alter management's decision if the concession necessary placed their wage below the opportunity wage.

The likelihood that bargaining would lead the employer to alter its decision also is problematic. What is the reason for the decision to close? Is it loss of raw materials, a shrinking market, labor costs or greater opportunities elsewhere? All of these could be termed economic reasons, but they differ in their suitability to change through bargaining. Another consideration is the bargaining history of these parties. Have they shown an ability to reach agreement in the past on troublesome issues?

The countervailing management interest in not bargaining is the most frequently alluded to, yet the least explained. Dire financial distress may force the firm to close, but the firm should have some indication of its worsening financial condition prior to the actual decision. Strategic plans to alter the nature of the business also are undertaken prior to any decision to close. Decisions to enter new markets may require greater secrecy, but those decisions would require bargaining only if a line of business was being discontinued. Management's interest in not bargaining appears to be grounded in (a) the uncertainty of the length of bargaining required to bargain in good faith, and (b) the ideological position that certain decisions are exclusively management prerogatives.

Rule of Rebuttable Presumption

The rule of rebuttable presumption was proposed in the U.S. Court of Appeals for the Second Circuit in its decision in *National Labor Relations Board v. First National Maintenance Corporation.*[2] The following passage from this decision is a statement of that rule.

> We believe, however, that the critical question is whether the purposes of the statute are advanced by imposition of a duty to bargain and that determination does not depend solely on whether the costs precipitating the decision to terminate were not labor originated. What appears to us to be the decisive factor, is whether, regardless of the origin of the cost which precipitated a management decision to terminate an operation, bargaining could reasonably be expected to modify or reverse that decision.[3]

This rule differs from the three part test of *Brockway* in which the interests of employers and employees are to be balanced. Rather, in the rebuttable presumption rule, the key concern is whether the purposes of the statute can be advanced.

Heinsz (1981) has attempted to formalize the rule of rebuttable presumption and to make it operational as it applies to plant closing. He specified six steps, which are as follows:

1. The initial presumption is that the decision to close is a mandatory subject of bargaining.

2. If the employer fails to bargain over the decision to close, the employer bears the burden of proving that the primary reason for closing was economic necessity outside the employment relation.

3. If the employer has avoided all bargaining and has failed to present evidence overcoming the presumption in favor of negotiations, the National Labor Relations Board should order back pay from the date of refusal to bargain.

4. If the employer has bargained before announcing the closing decision, it should be presumed that he has fulfilled his duty to bargain.

5. The presumption of having fulfilled the duty to bargain will be nullified if the bargaining has been done in bad faith, e.g., providing insufficient advance notice for the bargaining to affect the decision to close.

6. The union also has the obligation to bargain in good faith. That is, it should bargain in recognition of concluding the negotiation in a timely fashion and treating all data provided by the employer as confidential.

The rule of rebuttable presumption also appears to have some promise, but initial implementation would be difficult. Initially, Point 2 would be the subject of contention as both employers and employees would disagree over whether the primary reason for closing was outside the employment relation. For instance, assume the firm is closing the plant because its costs of production are too high in order to remain competitive. One approach is to build a new plant with state of the art technology. The other approach is to reduce the costs of labor inputs. Would the primary reason for closing be outside the employment relation?

Numerous observations would be necessary to develop the parameters of reasons of "economic necessity outside the employment relation." Initially, there would be no difference between the rule of rebuttable presumption and a simple mandatory duty to bargain, because the incentive would be to bargain due to the uncertainty of what reasons are acceptable and the high potential cost of not bargaining, as specified in Point 3.

Related to Point 3 is a concern that frequently emerges in the partial closure issue. Some assert that a case-by-case approach is necessary in order to be equitable to all—to maximize fairness; a *per se* rule is arbitrary because it does not distinguish among the various possible reasons for closing a plant. However, there is the potential in the case-by-case determination of the firm not knowing until after the judicial determination has been made whether the closure and the failure to bargain over the decision is legal. If illegal, the usual remedy—back pay to the date of closure—is extremely costly. But it appears that the costly remedy has been an underlying reason for not finding an unfair labor practice in some instances, when, in fact, an unfair practice has occurred.

In summary, each of the four rules reviewed here has a significant shortcoming. Schwarz's employment substitution rule would not require bargaining in plant closure cases. Rabin's seven point rule leaves the definition of "compelling factor" open, and specifying flexible interpretation of good faith bargaining does not necessarily reduce the uncertainty associated with meeting its requirements. The three part test of Brockway would still require case-by-case adjudication because determining the strength of the employees' interest requires negotiations; therefore, there still is extreme uncertainty associated with whether or not there is a duty to bargain. Finally, Heinsz's formalization of the rule of rebuttable presumption still leaves undefined what is "economic necessity outside the employment relation." Thus, other than Schwarz's rule, each of the rules still relies heavily on the case-by-case determination.

A New Proposal

The four alternatives presented in the previous section are designed to expedite the determination of whether there is a duty to bargain over the decision to close. In this section, I will present a new proposal. The proposal has its basis in Coase's (1971) concept of social costs and bargaining to reach a solution that is satisfactory to both parties and that maximizes the value of production. Initially, the concept of social cost is examined and its application to the plant closure problem is detailed. The new proposal is presented at the end of this section.

The concept of social cost is loosely defined. Coase used the following definition to introduce his discussion: "those actions of business firms which have harmful effects on others." One difficulty is making Coase's concept operational, given the practicalities of collective bargaining. The system of collective bargaining requires that (a) negotiations be expeditious and confidential, (b) relative bargaining power be maintained, and (c) penalties be costly enough to deter prohibited practices but are not so severe that they are never levied.

Coase's concept is based on the following five points.

1. The problem must be looked at in the total and at the margin.

2. The efficient allocation of resources and not necessarily the distribution of income is the fundamental issue.

3. The room for bargaining is between the resources' current use and their next best use.

4. The result which maximizes the value of production is independent of the legal position if the pricing system is assumed to work without cost.

5. The result is achieved by means of a bargain between the parties.

The potential harmful effect on workers, the social cost associated with plant closure, is their lost earnings. Earnings loss, however, is not a given, but depends on conditions in the local labor market, the compensation schedule used by the firm, and the preferences of workers and their tenure with the firm, as was discussed in chapter 2. Thus, depending on these factors, the potential earnings loss could be significant or negligible; but it is impossible to determine the extent of harmful effect on workers without negotiations.[4]

The other side of the issue is whether the action by the firm increases productive capacity of whether it is unavoidable. There is no room for bargaining if the closure is the only action possible. Bargaining, however, could address unexplored alternatives to closure. Finally, the action by the firm may be solely designed to maximize private profits, such as relocation to a lower wage area. Thus, alternatives for firms could be (a) closure because it is the only alternative, (b) closure although not all alternatives have been explored, and (c) relocation to a more profitable area or region.

Therefore, there are six potential combinations of the effect of closure on workers and the motivations of the firm. They are as follows:

1. Harmful effect on workers - No alternative to closure for the firm.

2. Harmful effect on workers - Alternatives to closure not explored.

3. Harmful effect on workers - More profitable opportunities for the firm.

4. No effect on workers - No alternative to closure for the firm.

5. No effect on workers - Alternatives to closure not explored.

6. No effect on workers - More profitable opportunities for the firm.

Decision bargaining is only meaningful when there is the potential of changing a closure decision. No such potential exists in 1 or 4. Although deferred compensation may be an issue in 1 or 4, the only reasonable option is to address it during "effects bargaining." In some instances, closure would not necessarily result in a loss of current earnings for a majority of the workers. The experience of workers under 40 cited by Holen (1981) fits this category.

"Alternatives to closure not explored" could include reasons ranging from low productivity or higher wages, to producing a product for which the market is shrinking, to loss of line of credit. In some circumstances closure could be averted but not in others. Bargaining also might improve the profitability of the current plant, making relocations less attractive. Thus, of the six possible interactions spelled out above, Coase's concept would suggest that there be an opportunity for "decision bargaining" in four of them, situations 2, 3, 5 and 6.

The following are two possible scenarios. Assume a plant announces that it is going to close. It is located in a relatively small local labor market. The reason for closing is loss of market share due to noncompetitive prices. Alternative job opportunities are limited and wages are 30 percent lower in those opportunities. The firm indicates that a 20 percent pay cut is necessary to retain competitiveness, and that figure is verified. Thus, the range of bargains is between a 30 percent and a 20 percent cut in pay. Workers agree to a 20 percent pay cut because it represents the best alternative. They have incurred an earnings loss, but that loss is less than it might have been, and the productive capacity has been maintained in the community. This represents the minimum social cost associated with maintaining production capacity.

The second scenario assumes that a plant announces that it is closing in order to relocate its facility to a low cost area. The local labor market affords numerous opportunities and most workers can obtain alternate employment and incur only a 10 percent cut in pay. The firm claims a 20 percent cut in pay plus significant technological changes are necessary in order to make the current location competitive. In this instance closure is the best alternative for both parties because resources can be reallocated to more productive uses without significantly damaging the earnings potential of workers.[5]

The discussion of the court cases and NLRB rulings has demonstrated that the courts generally have been willing to accept economic reasons as a justifiable circumstance for closing a plant or displacing a large part of the workforce. The term "economic reasons" is a bit contrived, however. For instance, closing a plant to avoid bargaining with a union is expected to generate economic benefits for the firm. Labor costs that are sufficiently high to make a firm noncompetitive also would appear to be an economic reason. Below are described the types of actions of firms that appear to constitute economic reasons according to the definitions of the courts.

1. A major capital investment. The capital investment could result in the displacement of a significant part of the workforce as the process becomes more automated. Presumably, the physical capital investment is undertaken to maintain or enhance the competitive position of the firm. The major capital investment also could take the form of a relocation.

2. Altering the line of work. By altering its line of work, the skills possessed by a significant part of the workforce and the skills required to produce the new product or service may no longer match. Stated differently, the firm has diversified to meet changing market conditions.

3. Loss of market. The loss of market, which results in closure, could be for several reasons.

   a. the firm is no longer competitive in its industry or market.

   b. the market for the product no longer exists because consumer demands have shifted.

   c. the firm loses its ability to produce for this market. It may have lost its line of credit or no longer have access to its natural resource base.

To these a fourth point is added which is:

4. The firm is no longer competitive because wages are too high, productivity is too low, or restrictive work rules impair flexibility.

If one takes a very narrow view of what bargaining can resolve, bargaining reasonably could be expected to generate a solution only in the fourth situation.

A more expansive view of issues that might be resolved through decision bargaining could also include the first point. For instance, a change in work rules or a decrease in wages could make a major capital investment less necessary.

Altering the line of work and changing the skill needs of workers, the second point, could be facilitated by bargaining over retraining programs for workers, but this is effects bargaining. The loss of a market is the one general area in which the potential impact of bargaining is expected to be quite limited.

Calabresi (1970) has attempted to develop liability rules that promote efficiency, which is defined as minimizing the sum of accident costs and accident prevention costs. Accident costs are those costs directly associated with the closure such as the earnings loss of workers. Accident prevention costs are those costs incurred to regulate or limit the occurrence of the accident.

Calabresi has concluded that the sum of accident costs and accident prevention costs would be minimized if liability for the costs was assigned to the party best able to affect the decision. If we consider a plant closure an accident, since costs are imposed on individuals not party to the decision, this would suggest that liability be assigned to the employer. The employer has the information—the reason for closure and what changes are necessary to avoid closure.[6]

If management has the necessary information, why not simply rely on management to initiate discussions when economic considerations can be altered through bargaining? Are they not in the best position to determine if there is something that labor can do to forestall the closure or displacement?

The question has merit, but it ignores several issues. First, whether the concessions demanded by the firm will increase productive capacity for society depends on the alternatives available and the preferences of the workers. The value of goods and services produced is less than that attainable if workers are not employed in their best alternative. Second, since both the worker and the firm have invested capital, is it equitable to permit only management to determine those cases in which bargaining should occur—to assign priority rights to physical capital? Firms and workers are unequally positioned to respond to change due to the time input requirement of human capital.[7] Third, where is the bargaining power for the union? The only power is the right to not agree, which would be very costly to exercise when the union is given only selective opportunities to participate in decision bargaining. Fourth, it ignores the potential of workers providing innovative ideas that may be effective in situations that management did not consider possible. Fifth, there is the fear that employers may misuse the threat of closure, using it to gain concessions in situations where there is no real potential for closure.

Placing the decision rather than obligation with management may result in fewer agreements being reached than desirable. Management does not know the union perfectly. It is not fully aware of the concessions the union will be willing to make, nor the internal political positioning of members. A concession that management may think the union would be willing to make may be rejected, whereas one they thought impossible may be agreed to readily. Moreover, not all plants should remain open. In some instances the economic sacrifice by employees would be greater than the improvement in productive capacity. Most important, closures are relatively infrequent, so the expected transactions cost is relatively small.

Although others have attempted to establish criteria for the duty to decision bargain, there is excessive uncertainty associated with case-by-case adjudication. Making Coase's concepts operational requires a *per se* rule: there is a mandatory duty to bargain over the decision to close a plant or relocate its operation. The key consideration is expeditiously determining when additional bargaining is warranted. The new proposal presented below attempts to have a quick determination of when additional bargaining could lead to a socially more productive solution than closure.

Recall that bargaining potentially could resolve the situation in four of the six combinations of effects of closure and motivations of firms. In the other two of the combinations, bargaining could not possibly alter the decision: closure is the only alternative. In two more of the combinations (2 and 5) some bargaining is necessary to explore the alternatives to closure. In some instances alternatives may be available, but not in others. Finally, bargaining is needed to explore the more profitable alternatives for the firm in light of the opportunities for workers. Consider the following procedure for implementing the duty to bargain over the decision to close a plant and for meeting this obligation:

1. Firms are required to notify the NLRB and the union of the plan to close one part of an operation or to relocate. This notice should contain a detailed explanation of the reasons for closure and financial data as appropriate.

2. The NLRB determines if bargaining might be fruitful using the criteria established in *Brooks-Scanlon;*[8] the reasons for closure are beyond the control of the parties to the collective bargaining agreement.

3. Information bargaining occurs in those instances where it is determined that bargaining might be fruitful.

4. Based on the information provided, the NLRB, the union or bargaining unit, and the firm determine whether further bargaining is appropriate.

5. Bargaining continues in those instances where two of the three (the NLRB, the union or bargaining unit, and the firm) think progress is being made and/or a solution is possible, but for no more than 90 days after the initial notice.

6. If bargaining has been in good faith, but no agreement is reached within the time period, the firm is free to proceed with its action.

7. The firm is required to bargain over the effects.

This proposal establishes a *per se* rule, but attempts to introduce steps that ensure that decision bargaining will not be required in circumstances where there is no reasonable chance of resolution. The proposal places a greater obligation on management than is currently required, but reduces uncertainty and the potential of costly penalties. The bargaining power of the union is limited, but is more than currently exists for effects bargaining.

One of the employer's concerns that surfaces is the uncertainty associated with meeting good faith bargaining requirements. The 90-day time limitation addresses this. The limitation should be absolute in order to discourage play-acting, and to promote bargaining.

The NLRB is charged with furthering the purposes of the National Labor Relations Act, which is to establish and maintain industrial peace to preserve the flow of commerce. It may be felt that the initial reaction of the Board will be that these purposes are best served by requiring bargaining in all situations, irrespective of the probability of changing the outcome. However, the Board, in its *Brooks-Scanlon* decision, has moved to the position that bargaining should not be required over the decision to close when there is no likelihood of reversing the decision. In *Brooks-Scanlon,* the firm lost its source of raw materials and the Board rejected a duty to bargain.

The proposal envisions a two step process. After initial bargaining has occurred, the progress will be reviewed to determine if a solution is likely. If none is likely, as indicated by two of the three parties agreeing so, further bargaining over the decision will not be required in order to meet good faith requirements. This second step would cover the situation where the market has changed so rapidly that the firm cannot possibly keep the plant open 90 days.

An important element of establishing a *per se* rule is that plant closure is a relatively infrequent event. Therefore, the additional costs of administering the proposal would be limited. Furthermore, it would use existing structures, but require that the National Labor Relations Act be amended to include plant closures and relocations as falling within the "terms and other conditions of employment."

Summary

Per se rules to guide the duty to bargain have been proposed because the judicial determination of the duty to bargain over closure is problematic. Perhaps the most troublesome aspect is that substantive labor law has been made in the area of plant closure through cases in which management and labor have never negotiated a contract. For example, neither Schwarz's nor Rabin's criteria would have required decision bargaining in the *First National Maintenance* decision.

One of the appealing features of using collective bargaining to help resolve the plant closure problem is that closure is a relatively infrequent event. As reported earlier, there were 619 closures in 1982, a year that has been compared to the Great Depression in terms of its impact on some sectors. Although the impact on the workers dislocated may be severe, the administrative impact for an agency such as the National Labor Relations Board should not be overly burdensome. For example, in fiscal year 1980, the NLRB handled over 44,000 unfair labor practice cases (Forty-fifth Annual Report of the NLRB, 1981).

Conversely, case-by-case determination can be extremely costly in the individual situation. Other *per se* proposals to accommodate the partial closing judicial conundrum have been reviewed. Each attempt is noteworthy, but each one is flawed. The two areas on which they seem to stumble is ensuring that the negotiations are expeditious and introducing certainty into who is required to bargain over the decision.

The proposal presented above requires decision bargaining, but sets a time limit to the bargaining. It establishes a *per se* rule, but envisions a quick determination if further bargaining would be fruitful. For example, closure due to the loss of market likely would lead to the quick determination that bargaining over the decision would be fruitless and would permit early negotiations over the effects.[9]

NOTES

1. *Fibreboard Paper Products Corporation v. National Labor Relations Board,* 85 S. Ct. 398, 405 (1964).

2. *National Labor Relations Board v. First National Maintenance Corporation,* 628 F.2d 596 (1980).

3. 627 F.2d 596, 602.

4. For the purposes of this monograph, earnings losses are divided into two components: (a) the difference in wages received between the position in the closed plant and the new job, and (b) the uncompensated deferred compensation.

5. Naturally, there may be short-run adjustment costs for workers associated with the closure. But the extent of opportunities should minimize the income loss, and therefore the adjustment costs.

6. Although one of Coase's five points held that the efficient result is independent of the legal position if the pricing system is assumed to work without costs, that may not be the case due to the unequal distribution of information. Bargaining then becomes the mechanism for equalizing the distribution of information.

7. The importance of human capital to firms is evidenced by the fact that some service firms have issued stock. These firms do not produce goods in the traditional sense, so there is no physical capital—buildings, machines, inventories—which could be liquidated to generate some return to the shareholder. For example, consider investment houses or consulting firms. Some have gone public and shares in the company are being traded. The company may lease space and have no inventory, although it may have a portfolio of stocks. In actuality, the values of the shares of stock are based on the human capital of the individuals employed by the company. Thus, one must question the preoccupation of the Courts with physical capital.

8. *Brooks-Scanlon, Inc. v. Local 1017, Lumber and Sawmill Workers,* 102 LRRM 1606 (1979).

9. A difficult feature of the proposal is that it does not accommodate the *Adams Dairy* problem. The establishment continues, but a subset of workers is replaced. Do we continue to rely on *Fibreboard* or do we attempt to bring this situation under the proposal?

Chapter 5

Plant Closure Protections and the Collectively Bargained Contract

Introduction

When a plant is closed or a large scale dislocation occurs, certain protections may be in place or may have been provided for workers to ease the transition between jobs. Severance pay, usually a lump sum, may be paid to those who have stayed until the plant is closed. Supplemental unemployment benefits (SUB) may have been negotiated to augment unemployment compensation. Job search or relocation assistance may be provided or advance notice of the closure or dislocation may have been given. Other workers may have secured the right to transfer to a new facility or obtained preferential hiring rights in those instances when the closure actually represents a relocation of the production facilities of the plant.

Several decisions of the U.S. Supreme Court have referenced the incidence of negotiated provisions in the contract. In *Fibreboard Paper Products Corporation v. National Labor Relations Board,* the finding that a significant number of contracts included provisions limiting the ability of firms to contract out work was an important piece of evidence in leading the Supreme Court to rule that subcontracting was a mandatory topic of bargaining. In *First Na-*

tional Maintenance Corporation v. National Labor Relations Board, the U.S. Supreme Court used the fact that provisions requiring management to bargain with the union over the decision to close, or similar decisions, were relatively rare as an indication that mandatory bargaining over these decisions was not warranted. Instead, the greater frequency of bargaining over advance notice, interplant transfer and relocation, and other "effects" issues indicated to the court that "effects bargaining" and not "decision bargaining" was more appropriate. Therefore, the extent of bargaining over plant closure is important not only as an indicator of the number of workers covered, but also of how changes in the extent of bargaining may portend adjustments to judicial interpretations.

Why individual contracts contain some plant closure provisions and others do not may go beyond differences in sheer bargaining power. There are economic incentives involved in these types of protections for both management and labor. The purpose of this chapter is to examine these incentives for bargaining over plant closure. The first general question concerns the incidence of bargaining over the contractual protections. The second question concerns whether the inclusion of these protections is a response to changed realities about employment security. Specifically, have management and labor used formal contract negotiations to obtain protections and to develop solutions for workers and firms "at risk of closure?"

Incentives Associated With Plant Closure Provisions

Severance Pay

Severance pay is the compensation given to a worker who is terminated. The connotation associated with it is that the leaving is involuntary and perhaps unexpected. For example, severance pay is given to workers who are let go where sions are paid to workers who retire. The usual presumption is that severance pay is given to ease the pain and to tide the workers over until something new can be found following the involuntary separation. However, severance pay also can be used as a deterrent to closure.

Because severance pay is multifaceted, it may be the most desirable contractual provision covering plant closure from the union's perspective. (As was shown in chapter 2, increasing severance payments due workers may reduce the probability that a firm will close one plant in order to relocate to a new location.) This conjecture is consistent with the finding (reported below) that severance pay is the most frequently negotiated contract provision of this group.

Supplemental Unemployment Benefits

Supplemental unemployment benefits (SUB) are payments to workers who are separated from their jobs, either temporarily or permanently. This is a payment in addition to the benefits received through the unemployment insurance system of the state. However, rather than being part of a pool of firms in which some cross subsidization occurs, the program is funded directly by the firm. The cost of the program is borne by the firm that is laying off the workers or closing the operation.

Just as with severance pay, SUB increases the costs to the firm of shutting down an operation. By the same token, SUB benefits are likely to be available only to those employees who are terminated or who remain with the firm until closure, and not to those who leave voluntarily. For the worker, it also provides an extra financial cushion such that the loss of employment does not result in a drastic drop in income, and permits greater selectivity in searching for a new position. Because SUB payments generally are available to most workers in a union, there is not likely to be the conflict in union bargaining goal determination between more senior and less senior workers.

Advance Notice

One issue at the heart of the plant closure policy debate is whether a firm should be required to provide advance notice of the closing. Workers assert that advance notice is necessary so that (a) they may investigate options to save their jobs, (b) they have time to adjust psychologically to the loss of their job, and (c) they may begin the search for a new job immediately in order to minimize the period of unemployment and the potential wage loss. Firms, on the other hand, have tended to oppose advance notice arguing that (a) employee morale and productivity would be reduced, (b) employees would leave so the firm would be unable to fill its final orders, and (c) employees would sabotage the plant and equipment, therefore reducing the value of these assets.

What are some of the potential costs associated with providing advance notice? All of the reasons provided above are somewhat speculative. Will employee productivity decline? Will the attrition of workers increase? Will workers sabotage plant and equipment? For instance, consider employee productivity. Employee productivity tends to decline as the economy enters the downturn of a business cycle in order to make the work last as long as possible before layoffs begin. Weber and Taylor (1963), in their classic article on plant closure, indicated that this problem had not developed in the plant closings they studied. But this must still be considered a real possibility, because there appears to be the potential for increased costs due to reduced productivity.

Another source of costs would be if advance notice increased the quit rate above the normal level of attrition.

There are fixed costs associated with hiring and training new workers, or retraining existing workers, so if advance notice increased the quit rate, the firm would experience an increase in costs. But the impact on the quit rate is likely to be a function of the reasons for closure. If the closure is due to cyclical circumstances either for the industry or the economy, workers may not quit because there are fewer opportunities available. If the closure is due to circumstances specific to the firm, attrition may increase, and therefore there would be additional hiring, training, or retraining costs for the firm.

The issue of sabotage probably is most speculative; as Weber and Taylor (1963) also found, "all reports indicate that this problem has not developed." (p. 312)

The greatest benefits of advance notice probably are in the potential to avert closure. With advance notice, the union may have the opportunity to propose alternatives that might keep the plant open, that is, to engage in "decision bargaining." However, resistance to this may occur since this could give workers a foothold in an area traditionally reserved as a management right. The benefit derived from the opportunity to adjust psychologically to the loss of employment is obvious, although not necessarily quantifiable. Since severance pay and supplemental unemployment benefits generally require staying until closure, it is questionable whether the advance notice would be used to engage in labor market search. Advance notice might be more beneficial to workers when displaced worker programs are available.

Relocation and/or Transfer Rights

Relocation and/or transfer rights provide the potential for employment continuity with the same firm, albeit at a different location. They differ from the other plant closure provisions in that they are not necessarily deterrents to the firm.

Facing a requirement to relocate its workforce could deter a firm from closing one plant and opening another elsewhere; but one could suggest that the firm also might desire this type of provision, particularly if its labor force is specially skilled. It is expected that these provisions would be more prevalent in single-firm, multiple plant operations or industries that have faced changing geographical markets for their products.[1]

The Frequency of Plant Closure Provisions

The frequency of key plant closure provisions in major collective bargaining agreements is presented in this section. Two major comparisons are made: (1) frequency by region, and (2) frequency by "right-to-work" status of the state. The first comparison is made because there is the presumption that establishments in the Northeast and Midwest are more likely to be losing employment and that the plants are at greater risk of being closed.

The second comparison is made because states have used their right-to-work status as an indicator that unions are less powerful and that the collective bargaining environment is more favorable to management. Right-to-work laws essentially limit a union's right to negotiate a union security clause which requires workers to pay periodic dues and initiation fees as a condition of employment. Such a clause is considered crucial to a union's strength because it enhances the financial resources the union can count on and mitigates the potential "free-rider" problem.[2]

The key plant closure provisions are advance notice of shutdown (SHUTDWN), relocation allowances (RELOCATE), transfer rights (TRANPLT), preferential hiring rights (TRANHIRE), a combination of transfer rights and hiring rights (TRANCOMB), severance pay

(SEVRANCE), supplemental unemployment benefits (SUB), and advance notice of technological change (CHANGE).

The data source is the United States Department of Labor's file of contracts covering more than 1,000 workers in effect in 1974, and the contracts covering more than 1,000 workers in effect in 1980. These contracts were negotiated principally in 1971, 1972 and 1973, and in 1977, 1978 and 1979, respectively. Only those agreements in the manufacturing sector (SIC 200 through SIC 399) were used. After editing the data and limiting the analysis to just those contracts covering production workers, 631 contracts were available for analysis for 1974 and 676 for 1980. The Department of Labor coded the provisions in the contract, usually indicating the presence or absence of the provision. Due to the method of coding, the provisions have become homogeneous even through there may have been considerable variation in the way they were written or have been interpreted by the parties to the contract.

Table 5.1 provides a listing of the incidence of provisions related to plant closure by region in 1974. The same data for 1980 are presented in table 5.2.[3] The most frequently negotiated provision in 1974 was severance pay, which was included in as few as 24 percent of the contracts in the Pacific region to as many as 47 percent of the Interstate contracts. Interstate contracts cover establishments in more than one state. Since severance pay usually is a money payment to employees who have been terminated and since termination can occur for a variety of reasons, severance pay protection is not exclusively a plant closure provision.

Supplemental unemployment benefits (SUB) tended to be the second most frequently negotiated provision. It was most common in the Interstate contracts (39 percent) and least common in those contracts covering establishments in the

Table 5.1
Percentage of Major Contracts Containing Plant Closure
Related Provisions in 1974, by Region*

Provisions	Northeast (percent)	Midwest (percent)	South & Plains (percent)	Pacific (percent)	Interstate (percent
RELOCATE	4	8	2	4	31
TRANPLT	13	17	13	16	20
TRANHIRE	2	5	4	4	16
TRANCOMB	4	8	2	7	19
SEVRANCE	40	43	36	24	47
SUB	23	27	14	10	39
SHUTDWN	11	12	14	16	20
CHANGE	12	6	11	9	12
Total contracts	166	160	160	70	75

SOURCE: Computer run from *Characteristics of Major Collective Bargaining Agreements, 1974.*

*The states grouped in the following regions:

Northeast: Maine, New Hampshire, Vermont, Massachusetts, Rhode Island, Connecticut, New York, New Jersey, Pennsylvania.

Midwest: Ohio, Indiana, Illinois, Michigan, Wisconsin.

South & Plains: Minnesota, Iowa, Missouri, North Dakota, South Dakota, Nebraska, Kansas, Delaware, Maryland, District of Columbia, Virginia, West Virginia, North Carolina, South Carolina, Georgia, Florida, Kentucky, Tennessee, Alabama, Mississippi, Arkansas, Louisiana, Oklahoma, Texas, Montana, Idaho, Wyoming, Colorado, New Mexico, Arizona, Utah, Nevada.

Pacific: Washington, Oregon, California, Alaska, Hawaii.

Table 5.2
Percentage of Major Contracts Containing Plant Closure
Related Provisions in 1980, by Region

Provisions	Northeast (percent)	Midwest (percent)	South & Plains (percent)	Pacific (percent)	Interstate (percent
RELOCATE	6	8	5	9	34
TRANPLT	15	21	22	24	17
TRANHIRE	3	5	6	7	20
TRANCOMB	4	8	2	5	23
SEVRANCE	40	34	38	32	47
SUB	19	31	13	11	55
SHUTDWN	12	9	16	16	24
CHANGE	13	6	14	8	13
Total contracts	160	155	172	74	115

SOURCE: Computer run from *Characteristics of Major Collective Bargaining Agreements, 1980*.

Pacific region (10 percent). Provisions providing relocation allowances and preferential hiring rights were the least frequently negotiated for those contracts covering establishments in any of the four distinct regions. However, relocation allowance was a relatively common provision in the Interstate contracts.

Given the usually strong opposition to legislative proposals with advance notice requirements, the presumption is that significant union bargaining power is required to obtain them. The stronger, more aggressive unions are concentrated in the Midwest. Thus, it is somewhat paradoxical that the advance notice provisions are slightly more frequent in the South & Plains. This issue is addressed more rigorously later in this chapter.

Contract outcomes related to plant closure in 1980 were characterized by significant changes in the incidence of both severance pay and transfer rights provisions. Specifically, the incidence of severance pay provisions dropped 9 percentage points between 1974 and 1980 in contracts covering establishments in the Midwest, but increased 8 percentage points in contracts in the Pacific regions. There also was a marked increase in most regions in the incidence of transfer rights between 1974 and 1980. For instance, there was a 9 percentage point increase in the frequency of TRANPLT in the South & Plains region and an 8 percentage point increase in the Pacific region. One explanation is that this increase may have been a response to the fear of industrial relocation. On the other hand, given the reluctance of workers to relocate, this provision may be a low-cost concession for firms, thereby increasing its frequency.

T-tests were conducted to determine if the differences between regions in the frequency that these provisions were included in the contracts were statistically significant. For the 1974 file, the only statistically significant difference between the Northeast and the South & Plains was for the SUB provision. Only the incidence of transfer rights was significantly different between these two regions in 1980.

In 1974, differences in the frequency of contract provisions, relocation allowance, a combination of transfer rights and preferential hiring rights, and supplemental unemployment benefits in the contracts covering establishments in the Midwest versus the South & Plains were statistically significant. The incidence of the three provisions was greater in the Midwest. However, by 1980, the incidence of advance notice of shutdown and advance notice of technological change also were significantly different between these regions, but these two provisions were more common in contracts covering establishments in the South & Plains.

The t-tests conducted involving the Northeast and the Pacific found statistically significant differences between these two regions in the frequency of severance and supplemental unemployment benefits in 1974, whereas in 1980, the only difference was in transfer rights, with the frequency being greater in the Pacific region.

The comparison of the Midwest with the Pacific followed a similar pattern. Specifically, there were statistically significant differences in the frequency of supplemental unemployment benefits and severance pay in 1974, but in 1980, the only difference in the contracts covering establishments in these two regions was the frequency of supplemental unemployment benefits.

The final step was to determine if there were any statistically significant differences in the frequency of these contract provisions between the South & Plains region and the Pacific region. In 1974, the differences in the frequency of a combination of preferential hiring rights and transfer rights, and severance pay were statistically significant. In

1980, however, no statistically significant differences in these contract provisions emerged.

The expectations concerning contractual provisions related to plant closure were based on the accepted cliché that manufacturing establishments in the Northeast and Midwest had been losing employment. However, an examination of production worker employment growth in those 3-digit industries represented in the major contracts file portrays a different picture.

As shown in table 5.3, the largest proportion of firms in industries with growth rates exceeding 25 percent in the 1967 to 1979 period were in the Midwest and Northeast. Fully 18.1 percent of the contracts in the Midwest covered establishments in industries where employment growth exceeded 25 percent in that period. Furthermore, only in the Midwest region were there more contracts in industries in which employment was growing rather than declining. Thus, the growth rate in plant closure provisions in contracts covering establishments in the South & Plains and the Pacific is quite consistent with relative employment growth in those regions.

Instead of separating the incidence of provisions by region, the states were grouped into right-to-work (RTW) states and states which do not have right-to-work laws. There were 19 states in 1974 that had right-to-work laws, and those states are listed in table 5.4.[4] Generally, right-to-work laws are an indicator of the political climate towards organized labor. Therefore, we would expect the frequency of plant closure provisions to be less in right-to-work states.[5]

As indicated in table 5.4, this expectation holds more for the contracts covering establishments in 1974 than for 1980. In fact, there is *no* difference statistically between these two groups of states in the frequency of provisions covering preferential hiring rights, transfer rights, severance pay, ad-

Table 5.3
Percent of Establishment by Industry's Manufacturing Growth Rates
Over the 1967 to 1979 Period for 3-Digit SIC Industries*

Manufacturing growth	Northeast (percent)	Midwest (percent)	South & Plains (percent)	Pacific (percent)	Interstate (percent
Greater than or equal to 25 percent	9.0	18.1	6.9	5.7	5.3
10 percent to 24 percent	18.7	15.0	17.5	22.9	20.0
0 percent to 9 percent	17.5	19.4	16.9	8.6	13.3
-9 percent to -1 percent	19.3	18.1	26.2	25.7	30.7
-24 percent to -10 percent	19.9	22.5	20.6	28.6	25.3
Less than or equal to -25 percent	15.7	6.9	11.9	8.6	5.3

SOURCE: Author's calculations based on data from the U.S. Department of Labor, Bureau of Labor Statistics, *Employment and Earnings, United States, 1909-1978* and *Supplement.* Washington, DC, Government Printing Office, 1978 and 1982.

*The 3-digit industries are those in which an establishment or establishments with more than 1,000 production workers are covered by a collective bargaining contract.

vance notice of plant closings and advance notice of major technological changes in either 1974 or 1980. Therefore, at least in the area of plant closure, the differential impact of unionization on contractual outcomes in the right-to-work states relative to the other states is minimal.

Table 5.4
Percentage of Major Contracts Containing Plant Closure
Related Provisions in 1974 and 1980, by Right-to-Work Status
of State in Which Establishment is Located**

	1974		1980	
Provisions	RTW (percent)	No RTW (percent)	RTW (percent)	No RTW (percent)
RELOCATE	0	6*	4	7
TRANPLT	13	15	21	22
TRANHIRE	1	4	6	4
TRANCOMB	1	6*	1	6*
SEVRANCE	33	39	35	37
SUB	8	23*	10	22*
SHUTDWN	10	14	16	12
CHANGE	10	10	12	10
Total contracts	104	452	113	448
Number of workers	207,100	1,217,250	231,400	1,029,300

SOURCE: Computer run from *Characteristics of Major Collective Bargaining Agreements, 1980.*

NOTE: Contracts classified as Interregional are not included in this analysis.

*Statistically significant difference in mean values at .10 percent level using a t-test.

**Right-to-Work states in 1974 were: Alabama, Arizona, Arkansas, Florida, Georgia, Iowa, Kansas, Mississippi, Nebraska, Nevada, North Carolina, North Dakota, South Carolina, South Dakota, Tennessee, Texas, Utah, Virginia, Wyoming.

Louisiana adopted a Right-to-Work law in 1976. New Hampshire has no Right-to-Work law statute, but a decision by the New Hampshire Supreme Court effectively provides the same requirements of a Right-to-Work law.

Several points need to be highlighted. Severance payments are the most frequently negotiated provision, both in right-to-work states and the other states. Severance payments serve a dual purpose. They provide income protection in the case of closure, but they also increase its cost. There also has been a substantial growth in the incidence of interplant transfer rights. Between 1974 and 1980, the proportion of contracts including interplant transfer rights increased 8 percentage points and 7 percentage points in right-to-work states and the other states, respectively.

One of the difficulties of analyzing collective bargaining contracts is that there is a need to place provisions into categories, yet this assumes that similar provisions are homogeneous across contracts, when in fact they are not. For instance, one contract may provide for a $500 relocation allowance and another contract may require a $1,000 relocation allowance. According to the framework used thus far, the contracts simply would be categorized as having a relocation allowance provision. Yet the differences in the provisions covering relocation could indicate significant differences in bargaining power, industry conditions, et cetera. Unfortunately, when using the population of contracts covering 1,000 workers or more, which already has been coded by the U.S. Department of Labor, it is not possible to recognize the heterogeneity of most contract provisions. Nor is it usually practical to attempt to account for these differences in statistical analyses.

Two instances in which this is possible are advance notice of plant closure (SHUTDWN) and advance notice of technological change (CHANGE). The provisions have been coded according to the number of days of advance notice that is to be given. Table 5.5 provides this information for SHUTDWN and similar data for CHANGE is provided in table 5.6.

As shown in table 5.5, in 1974 the majority of the contracts did not specify the actual number of days of advance notice of closure. By 1980 greater specificity had been incorporated in the contract. Between 1974 and 1980 there was a substantial increase in the number of contracts and the number of workers covered specifying 1 to 30 days of advance notice. In 1974, 12 contracts covering over 23,000 workers had provisions requiring 1 to 30 days of notice. By 1980 there were 19 contracts covering more than 112,000 workers requiring this length of notice. There also was a doubling in the number of contracts and workers covered receiving 61 to 90 days of notice of closure over the six years.

Table 5.5
Variations in Advance Notice
of Closure (SHUTDWN) Provisions
1974 and 1980

	1974		1980	
Length of notice	**Contracts**	**Workers**	**Contracts**	**Workers**
1 to 30 days	12	23,650	19	112,250
31 to 60 days	7	47,950	7	47,050
61 to 90 days	7	14,750	14	30,350
91 days or more	12	37,150	13	40,400
Notice, but unspecified	49	220,990	47	172,350
Total contracts with advance notice	87	344,490	100	402,400

SOURCE: Computer run from *Characteristics of Major Collective Bargaining Agreements, 1974* and *1980*.

Provisions providing for advance notice of technological change were even less specific than those described above. In both 1974 and 1980, almost 60 percent of the major contracts including advance notice of technological change did not specify the length of advance notice. The largest share of contracts that did specify length provided between 1 to 30 days notice. The paucity of contracts covering technological change is quite surprising. Not only is there the more recent interest in the impact of technological change, but the late

1950s and early 1960s were influenced by the automation scare. The Manpower Development and Training Act of 1962 initially was targeted to workers impacted by technological change. Thus, one would have anticipated greater sensitivity to this issue.

Table 5.6
Variations in Advance Notice
of Technological Change (CHANGE) Provisions
1974 and 1980

Length of notice	1974		1980	
	Contracts	Workers	Contracts	Workers
1 to 30 days	19	78,300	20	78,950
31 to 60 days	1	3,500	3	7,750
61 to 90 days	4	11,400	7	16,150
91 days or more	1	3,300	1	1,650
Notice, but unspecified	37	210,300	44	579,750
Total contracts with advance notice	62	306,800	75	684,250

SOURCE: Computer run from *Characteristics of Major Collective Bargaining Agreements, 1974* and *1980.*

Provisions designed to mitigate the problems arising from plant closure are not widespread in major collective bargaining agreements. The two most frequently negotiated provisions, SEVRANCE and SUB, however, are not exclusively "closure" or "significant technological change" provisions. There also is considerable variation in the frequency of the eight provisions. Between 1974 and 1980, there was a marked increase in the frequency of only one provision, transfer rights (TRANPLT). One unanticipated finding is that differences in these bargaining outcomes among the regions are disappearing.

Contract provisions do not have to be widespread, however, to suggest that bargaining is moving toward solutions and protections. All that is necessary is that the population at risk has obtained such protections. Determining whether this has occurred is the subject of the next section.

The Determinants of Plant Closure Provisions in Formalized Negotiations

The objective of this section is to investigate the determinants of the inclusion of provisions addressing plant closure or permanent dislocation of workers in the formally bargained contracts in effect in 1974 and 1980. The underlying hypothesis is that changes in bargaining outcomes are responses to long-run changes in the structure of manufacturing and in the location of economic activity. Through this analysis it is hoped that the following question can be answered: Have management and labor used formal contract negotiations to obtain protections and to develop solutions for workers and firms at risk of closure? "At risk of closure" is defined in two ways. In the first instance, it is those industries in which production worker employment declines have been relatively great. In the second instance it is those industries in which the rate of plant closure has been relatively high.

Much has been made of the "concession bargaining" that occurred in a number of key negotiations in 1981 and 1982. The one side of concession bargaining has been the union givebacks of wages and/or fringe benefits. The other side is that, in a number of these negotiations, management has conceded employment security guarantees and greater input in plant closure decisions. Kassalow (1983) indicates that new protections, such as improvements in severance pay, supplementary unemployment plans and transfer rights, were gained by unions during the 1981-82 period of concession bargaining in exchange for waiving future benefits. The Bureau of National Affairs, Inc. (1983) reported that 50 of the 203 concessionary agreements provided explicit employment security guarantees and 9 of these contracts gave the unions a say in company decisions. Kassalow also notes that unions not under pressure to make concessions obtained advance notice provisions for plant closure or transfer of work while negotiating substantial improvements in the economic conditions of their employment.

Establishing the determinants of plant closure provisions can indicate which workers have either the greatest taste for the protection afforded by these provisions or consider themselves most at risk to be affected by closure. Establishing the determinants also should demonstrate which workers have the bargaining power necessary to obtain these protections.

However, the concession negotiations of 1981-1982 may not be indicative of labor-management relations in the long run. Establishing the determinants of these outcomes under less severe circumstances, the 1970s, may provide a better understanding of the underlying conditions and motivations. The 1970s also was a period, as Cappelli (1983) has noted, in which import penetration was increasing and union representation was decreasing in a number of industries. The economy was stagnating. Union success in certification elections decreased precipitously relative to the 1960s (Prosten 1979). The average size of manufacturing plants in the *largest* Fortune 500 firms decreased from 895 to 855 employees and, more important, the average size of the new plants they opened was only 307 employees (Schmenner 1983).

Because of these factors, the distinct difference between employment reductions due to cyclical factors and those due to large scale reductions or plant closure should have become more apparent. As Mitchell (1983) has indicated, traditional employment security provisions protect senior workers from cyclical reductions but not from plant closure. Since senior employees are more likely to be involved in developing union bargaining policy objectives, union policy should have become more sensitive to the threat of closure or large scale reductions during the 1970s.

Conceptual Framework

The underlying premise of this research is that contract provisions over plant closure are scarce resources. Therefore, an economic choice in addition to the expenditure of bargaining capital is involved in their inclusion in negotiated contracts. Economic choice not only entails deciding whether to attempt to bargain over plant closure provisions, it also includes deciding over which provisions to bargain.

There are general trends in the economy that impact workers and to which some response is expected. For example, the rapid inflation of the second half of the 1970s increased the pressure for cost-of-living adjustments. Similarly, it is hypothesized that significant employment declines and the increased attention given to the problems arising from plant closure would sensitize workers to the need for contractual protections. Since contract provisions are scarce resources, it is expected that the workers in those industries and locations undergoing the greatest structural changes (shifting demand for their labor) would be willing to make the tradeoffs required to obtain these provisions.[6]

Based on this scenario, the following hypotheses are considered.

1. Variations in the incidence of provisions addressing permanent job dislocation in individual contracts should be negatively related to variations in employment growth across manufacturing industries, holding other factors constant.

2. Variations in the incidence of provisions addressing permanent job dislocation should be positively related to variations in the percent of plants closed in that industry, holding other factors constant.

3. Since plant closure provisions place a cost on the employer, the union's ability to obtain plant closure provisions depends on the strength of the union. Thus, variations in the incidence of contract provisions should be positively related to the extent that the industry's workforce is covered by collective bargaining agreements and negatively related to the extent of union rivalry, holding other factors constant.

4. Since right-to-work (RTW) laws are a positive signal of a pro-business environment, contractual outcomes should vary negatively with whether the contract covers an establishment(s) in a state with a right-to-work statute, holding other factors constant.[7]

It is not possible in the data sets available to observe individual contracts over time due to limitations in the ability to track contracts. Therefore, cross-sectional analysis is conducted on each of the data sets. By examining relationships at two different long-run positions, we should be able to observe changes in the ultimate determinants of bargained outcomes during this period.

Although most of the research on collective bargaining outcomes has addressed wage levels and wage changes, several studies recently have been conducted on the determinants of other contract provisions such as cost-of-living clauses in bargained contracts (Hendricks and Kahn 1983; Ehrenberg et al. 1982), the bargaining structure (Hendricks and Kahn 1982) and the correlates of general bargaining outcomes (Kochan and Block 1977).

One of the main difficulties in examining bargaining outcomes other than wages is that the outcome is not easily quantifiable. Furthermore, it is the expectation that these provisions are particularly sensitive to the characteristics of the workers in the bargaining unit. Some years ago, Sayles and Strauss (1952) found that bargaining units with older workers tended to seek pension benefits through collective bargaining whereas units with younger workers tended to seek health insurance coverage. Since we seldom know the demographic characteristics of the bargaining unit, calibration of the demand for nonwage provisions is more difficult. Not only is it difficult to obtain the demographic characteristics of the bargaining unit, union bargaining goal determination moves us into the realm of voting behavior and the power of relative interest groups within an organization (Farber 1978).

One other problem that plagues research on the determinants of bargaining outcomes is that the main hypothesis—the response of workers to a condition affecting their employment prospects—really is an attempt to model the propensity to negotiate over an issue. However, since only outcomes are observed, we may not be measuring the actual responsiveness of the union. Negotiating over these types of protections does not assure that they will be included in the final contract—hence, the need to emphasize the relative bargaining power of the union and the political environment for collective bargaining.

Data and Methodology

The basic sources of data were the U.S. Department of Labor's files of major collective bargaining agreements in effect for 1974 and 1980. These files include all major agreements in effect in the respective years. The major agreements are limited to those covering more than 1,000 workers. Only those agreements in the manufacturing sector

(SIC 200 through SIC 399) were used. After editing the data and limiting the analysis to just those contracts covering production workers, the number of contracts available for analyses were 631 for 1974 and 676 for 1980.

Eight contract provisions were categorized as addressing the permanent worker displacement issue. They were: (a) relocation allowances (RELOCATE), (b) transfer rights (TRANPLT), (c) preferential hiring rights (TRANHIRE), (d) a combination of b and c (TRANCOMB), (e) severance pay (SEVRANCE), (f) supplemental unemployment benefits (SUB), (g) advance notice of plant shutdown (SHUTDWN), and (h) advance notice of technological change (CHANGE).

The Department of Labor also coded the structure of the bargaining relationship, single firm-single plant (PLANT), single firm-multiple plant (MULTI), industry (INDUS), association (ASSOC); the number of workers covered by the contract (WORKERS); and the state in which the establishment is located. The state variable was used to segment the data by region and also to create a variable indicating whether or not the contract covered workers in a right-to-work state (RTW).

The structure of the bargaining relationship variables are primarily control variables, but there is an expected systematic relationship.[8] It is expected that multi-employer agreements result in less favorable agreements than single-employer agreements. The theoretical arguments lead to an ambiguous conclusion, but empirical work has shown that multi-employer outcomes lead to less favorable outcomes for unions (Kochan and Block 1977). However, if the negotiation is with a single firm, a firmwide agreement rather than a single plant agreement tends to be more advantageous for the union because it is not possible for the firm to whipsaw the union when all or most of the plants of an employer are covered in the same agreement.

The expectation for the coefficient of the number of workers is ambiguous. On the one hand, the greater the number of workers, the more resources the union is likely to have access to, which should enhance the union's ability to negotiate a more favorable bargain. On the other hand, management resistance to contract provisions may be increased as the number of workers covered increases.

Collective bargaining coverage (COV) at the 3-digit SIC level, a measure of union bargaining power, was taken from the estimates developed by Freeman and Medoff (1979). Their estimates of contract coverage were for 1968-1972 period.

Following Hendricks (1975), collective bargaining coverage also was measured by three dichotomous variables. Low coverage was defined as between 0 and 50 percent of the industry organized. Moderate coverage set the bounds at between 50 percent and 80 percent of the industry organized, and the high coverage dichotomous variable was assigned to those industries in which the percent covered by collective bargaining agreements exceeded 80 percent. The reasoning underlying this specification is that the relation between union bargaining power and coverage of industry does not increase in a smooth and continuous manner. Rather, there are critical levels of bargaining coverage beyond which a union's bargaining power changes by a disproportionate amount.

Changes in production worker employment (GROW74) and (GROW80) at the 3-digit SIC code for the periods 1967 to 1973 and 1973 to 1979, respectively, were calculated from *Employment and Earnings*.[9] These periods were chosen because each starting and ending year were near or at the peak of a cycle of economic activity. Consequently, the measured change in employment should be reflecting long-run structural influences as opposed to short run cyclical changes.

The probability of plant closure (CLOSE) is calculated as the ratio of the number of plants that were closed by Fortune 500 firms in the 1970s to the total number of plants at the start of the decade by 3-digit industries. This ratio was then multiplied by 100. This value was calculated from a computer printout provided by Roger Schmenner to the author. Schmenner's data set is based on his survey of Fortune 500 firms (see Schmenner 1982). However, it was not possible to calculate separate closure rates for the early part of the decade and for the latter part. Although the data used in the analysis is for 3-digit industries, an indication of the variation in closure rates across 2-digit industries is provided in table 5.7.[10] Closure rates varied from 20 percent of all plants in the leather and leather products industry to 3.0 percent in petroleum refining.

A variable that is included in several specifications is the length of the contract (LENGTH). As the contract length increases, greater risks are assumed by both sides. One of these risks is that changed market conditions could place the establishment and employment security in jeopardy. Although reopening a contract is possible, it generally requires the agreement of both parties. Thus, it is expected that more protections would be sought as the length of the contract increases.

Two other variables that were calculated are the degree of product market concentration at the 3-digit SIC level (CONC) and the extent of union rivalry (RIVAL). CONC was calculated as the weighted average value of the percent of shipments accounted for by the four largest companies in those 4-digit SIC industries comprising the 3-digit SIC.[11] The basic data were collected from the *Census of Manufactures* for both 1972 and 1977. CONC also was respecified as a set of dichotomous variables where low concentration, moderate concentration and high concentration were defined as ratios of 0-40 percent, 40-70 percent and 70-100 percent, respectively. The expected association between CONC and the dependent variable is ambiguous. Weiss (1966) asserted that it should be advantageous for the union to negotiate with firms in which the degree of product market concentration is high because these large firms will attempt to buy public favor by granting more union demands. Levinson (1967) argued that the large firms characteristic of concentrated industries have the financial resources to not grant union demands, but to incur long strikes.

RIVAL was calculated as the inverse of the number of unions negotiating major agreements at the 2-digit SIC, and therefore was derived from the 1974 and 1980 data sets. Increases in RIVAL represented increased concentration of major agreements with one union. The expected relationship is that as RIVAL rises, more resources are concentrated with the union, thereby increasing the union's ability to bargain more effectively.

The measures of employment growth, GROW74, GROW80, and the probability of closure (CLOSE) are indicators of expected job security. If employment in the industry declines, it may signify the increased probability that the establishment may close in the future, which should prompt the union to place provisions concerning closure as priority bargaining goals.[12] If a larger percent of plants close within an industry, it may indicate a structural shift such as increased foreign competition, which places all firms at risk. As indicated above, senior workers are not protected from job loss resulting from plant closure and the goals of senior workers tend to receive greater weights in the formation of union bargaining goals.

Table 5.7
Percentage of Plants Closed in Manufacturing Industries
in the 1970s by Fortune 500 Firms

Industry	Number of plants	Number closed	Percentage closed
Food & Kindred Products (20)	2,174	222	10.2
Tobacco Manufacturers (21)	32	1	3.1
Textile Mill Products (22)	383	36	9.4
Apparel (23)	267	24	9.0
Lumber & Wood Products (24)	401	30	7.5
Furniture & Fixtures (25)	183	23	12.6
Paper & Allied Products (26)	907	60	6.6
Printing & Publishing (27)	258	15	5.8
Chemicals & Allied Products (28)	1,739	119	6.8
Petroleum Refining (29)	397	12	3.0
Rubber Products (30)	494	38	7.7
Leather & Leather Products (31)	80	16	20.0
Stone, Clay, Glass & Concrete Products (32)	648	44	6.8
Primary Metals Industries (33)	603	49	8.1
Fabricated Metal Products (34)	947	89	9.5
Machinery, Except Electrical (35)	1,056	75	7.1
Electrical Machinery (36)	965	85	8.8
Transportation Equipment (37)	607	37	6.1
Scientific Instruments (38)	326	23	7.1
Miscellaneous Manufacturing (39)	212	23	10.8

SOURCE: Calculations based on computer printout provided by Roger Schmenner, August 16, 1983.

NOTE: Two-digit SIC code in parentheses.

The concern with right-to-work status of the state is it reflects that the division of political power between management and unions favors management, and that there are limits on unions' access to resources. All of these would suggest that the ability to obtain protections would be limited in these states.

The provisions were grouped into three categories and indices were developed for each category. An overall index also was calculated based on the eight provisions for each contract. Each provision was weighted equally in the construction of each index. The value of each index ranges between 0 and 100. The first index, INDEX1, is constructed from RELOCATE, TRANPLT, TRANHIRE and TRANCOMB. The second index, INDEX2, is constructed from SEVRANCE and SUB. The third index, INDEX3, is constructed from SHUTDWN and CHANGE. INDEX4 is constructed from all eight provisions. Indices of bargaining provisions have been used by other researchers, most notably Gerhart (1976) and Kochan and Block (1977).[13]

The associations are estimated using ordinary least squares (OLS) multiple regression analysis. Although OLS violates the assumptions of the best linear unbiased estimator, the estimates are consistent, and since the relationships primarily are associative and not necessarily causal, statistical significance rather than the exact marginal change is of greater interest. Furthermore, it has been shown that the improvement in the reliability of the estimates using alternate techniques such as logit or probit can be limited. (Werner, Wendling and Budde 1979)

Results

First Hypothesis: This hypothesis concerns whether the incidence of contract provisions addressing permanent job dislocation is directly related to negative employment growth in the industry in which the contract is negotiated. The key variables for testing this hypothesis are the percentage changes in production worker employment between 1967 and 1974 (GROW74), and between 1973 and 1979 (GROW80), respectively, in the three-digit industry. (It should be noted that contracts covering establishments in more than one state, interstate agreements, have been excluded from this phase of the analysis.)

The results for 1974 are listed in table 5.8 and the 1980 results are presented in table 5.9. Mean values and standard deviations for the variables are reported in table 5.10. The estimating equations explain only a relatively small percentage of the variation in the incidence of the contract provisions. As shown in table 5.8, the R-squared value ranges from .144 for INDEX1—relocation allowances, transfer rights—to .029 for INDEX3—advance notice of plant shutdown and technological change. GROW74 is of the hypothesized sign and statistically significant at conventional levels when INDEX3 and INDEX4 are the dependent variables for the 1974 analysis. Other findings of note are that collective bargaining coverage (COV) is positive and statistically significant for three of the tests, and the same finding holds for the number of workers covered (WORKERS). Thus the incidence of these provisions in contracts is strongly related to decreasing employment opportunities, size of the bargaining unit and collective bargaining coverage of the industry (union bargaining power).

The results for 1980 differed considerably, as is evident in table 5.9. GROW80 was not statistically significant in any of the analyses. Instead, variations in the incidence of plant closure provisions tended to be related to size of the bargaining unit, union bargaining power and the absence of rivals for the union. Perhaps as interesting a result is that the right-to-work dichotomous variable is not statistically significant in three of the four estimates. The presence of a right-to-work law usually is taken as a signal of a less favorable attitude towards unions. Yet, there does not appear to be a difference in bargained outcomes relating to plant closure depending on the presence or absence of a right-to-work law. Thus, on the basis of this analysis, there was only limited response to changed employment opportunities, and that response disappeared in the latter part of the 1970s.

Table 5.8
Determinants of the Incidence of Plant Closure Provisions
in Major Collectively Bargained Contracts, 1974
(standard errors in parentheses)

Independent variables	Dependent variable			
	INDEX1	INDEX2	INDEX3	INDEX4
GROW74	-.033	-.074	-.102*	-.060*
	(.033)	(.081)	(.059)	(.035)
RIVAL	-.011	.134	.110	.055
	(.044)	(.109)	(.080)	(.047)
CONC74	.057*	.099	.031	.061
	(.034)	(.084)	(.061)	(.036)
COV	.055*	.312*	-.027	.099*
	(.027)	(.068)	(.050)	(.029)
WORKERS (100s)	.037*	.100*	-.014	.040*
	(.015)	(.038)	(.028)	(.016)
RTW	-3.860*	-11.113*	-.650	-4.871*
	(1.420)	(3.521)	(2.576)	(1.516)
PLANT	2.009	-6.130	-5.792*	-1.975
	(1.792)	(4.441)	(3.249)	(1.912)
MULTI	10.844*	-8.504*	.554	3.434
	(1.978)	(4.903)	(3.588)	(2.111)
INDUS	1.396	-10.023	3.599	-.908
	(3.233)	(8.013)	(5.864)	(3.451)
INTERCEPT	-2.837	6.830	14.122	3.819
R-Squared	.144	.085	.029	.105
N	556			

*Statistically significant at .10 percent level (two-tailed test).

Table 5.9
Determinants of the Incidence of Plant Closure Provisions
in Major Collectively Bargained Contracts, 1980
(standard errors in parentheses)

Independent variables	Dependent variable			
	INDEX1	INDEX2	INDEX3	INDEX4
GROW80	.076	-.140	-.081	-.017
	(.052)	(.111)	(.082)	(.050)
RIVAL	-.005	.221*	.526*	.189*
	(.055)	(.118)	(.087)	(.053)
CONC80	.030	.165*	-.113*	.028
	(.038)	(.081)	(.059)	(.036)
COV	.051*	.260*	-.004	.089*
	(.031)	(.067)	(.050)	(.030)
WORKERS (100s)	.068*	.093*	.042	.068*
	(.022)	(.047)	(.034)	(.021)
RTW	-1.091	-7.443*	1.952	-1.918
	(1.599)	(3.415)	(2.516)	(1.549)
PLANT	3.044	-3.594	1.072	.891
	(2.095)	(4.477)	(3.298)	(2.030)
MULTI	8.585*	-1.215	4.394	5.087*
	(2.250)	(4.808)	(3.542)	(2.180)
INDUS	7.502*	-.893	9.584*	5.924
	(3.648)	(7.794)	(5.742)	(3.534)
INTERCEPT	-1.437	-1.405	6.134	1.416
R-Squared	.074	.070	.093	.080
N	561			

*Statistically significant at .10 percent level (two-tailed test).

Table 5.10
Mean Values and Standard Deviations of Variables
1974 and 1980
(standard deviations in parentheses)

	Year	
Variables	**1974**	**1980**
GROW74, GROW80	-8.62	2.03
	(16.57)	(12.28)
CLOSE	7.90	7.90
	(4.57)	(4.74)
RIVAL	13.58	13.58
	(12.45)	(11.91)
COV	69.87	71.25
	(22.23)	(22.50)
WORKERS (100s)	25.61	22.47
	(35.48)	(28.24)
CONC74, CONC80	37.52	37.90
	(17.88)	(18.30)
RTW	.18	.20
	(.39)	(.40)
PLANT	.61	.60
	(.48)	(.48)
MULTI	.21	.21
	(.40)	(.41)
INDUS	.03	.03
	(.18)	(.18)
INDEX1	6.92	8.91
	(13.47)	(14.96)
INDEX2	28.86	28.07
	(32.30)	(31.91)
INDEX3	11.24	11.76
	(22.94)	(23.80)
INDEX4	13.48	14.41
	(14.06)	(14.55)
Number of contracts	556	561

The most interesting results relate to INDEX3, the measurement of the incidence of advance notice of shutdowns or technological change. These provisions probably have been the most frequently mentioned in policy discussions of plant closure. They also most directly address the question of management rights.[14] The equation, particularly for 1974, explains a very small percentage of the total variation. The industry's growth rate was negatively related to the frequency as hypothesized; but union bargaining power was not statistically significant. Thus, there is very little insight into what features of the bargaining relationships or environments have resulted in approximately 15 percent of the contracts containing these provisions.

Second Hypothesis: This hypothesis addresses whether the incidence of contract provisions relating to plant closure is positively related to variations in the rate of plant closures across industries. Recall that the closure rates reported in table 5.7 ranged from 3.0 percent in the petroleum industry to 20.0 percent in the leather and leather products industry. Closure rates vary by industry because changes in consumer demands, foreign competition and other factors associated with structural change do not affect all industries to the same degree.

The percent of plants closed by Fortune 500 firms by 3-digit industry (CLOSE) was substituted for the employment growth measures in the estimating equation of the four indices. The results for 1974 and 1980 are reported in table 5.11 and table 5.12, respectively.

CLOSE is not statistically significant in any of the specifications, and the sign generally is negative, which is counter to expectations. The statistical insignificance of CLOSE is quite surprising. The frequency of plant closure in the industry should be a reasonably good indicator of the "at risk" potential for the workers and the bargaining unit.

Table 5.11
Determinants of the Incidence of Plant Closure Provisions in Major Collectively Bargained Contracts, 1974
(standard errors in parentheses)

Independent variables	Dependent variable			
	INDEX1	INDEX2	INDEX3	INDEX4
CLOSE	-.164	.265	-.090	-.171
	(.121)	(.302)	(.221)	(.130)
RIVAL	-.014	.124	.092	.047
	(.043)	(.108)	(.079)	(.046)
CONC74	.049	.086	.030	.053
	(.034)	(.086)	(.060)	(.037)
COV	.050*	.302*	-.034	.092*
	(.027)	(.068)	(.050)	(.029)
WORKERS (100s)	.040*	.106*	-.007	.045*
	(.015)	(.038)	(.028)	(.016)
RTW	-3.678*	-10.749*	-.268	-4.593*
	(1.416)	(3.513)	(2.576)	(1.514)
PLANT	2.305	-5.595	-5.403*	-1.596
	(1.795)	(4.452)	(3.266)	(1.919)
MULTI	11.140*	-7.925	1.124	3.870*
	(1.973)	(4.894)	(3.590)	(2.109)
INDUS	1.899	-9.138	4.168	-.292
	(3.242)	(8.040)	(5.898)	(3.466)
INTERCEPT	-1.153	9.570	15.117	2.740
R-Squared	.145	.085	.024	.103
N	556			

*Statistically significant at .10 percent level (two-tailed test).

Table 5.12
Determinants of the Incidence of Plant Closure Provisions
in Major Collectively Bargained Contracts, 1980
(standard errors in parentheses)

Independent variables	Dependent variable			
	INDEX1	INDEX2	INDEX3	INDEX4
CLOSE	-.089	.121	-.161	-.055
	(.142)	(.303)	(.223)	(.137)
RIVAL	-.006	.242*	.532*	.190*
	(.055)	(.118)	(.086)	(.053)
CONC80	.023	.175	-.124*	.024
	(.039)	(.084)	(.062)	(.038)
COV	.050	.259*	-.012	.087*
	(.032)	(.068)	(.050)	(.031)
WORKERS (100s)	.070*	.088*	.041	.067*
	(.022)	(.047)	(.034)	(.021)
RTW	-1.268	-7.081*	2.354	-1.816
	(1.596)	(3.409)	(2.510)	(1.544)
PLANT	3.666*	-4.701	.622	.813
	(2.069)	(4.418)	(3.252)	(2.000)
MULTI	8.994*	-1.963	3.982	5.002*
	(2.237)	(4.779)	(3.518)	(2.164)
INDUS	7.879*	1.418	10.170*	6.127*
	(3.694)	(7.890)	(5.808)	(3.573)
INTERCEPT	-.601	1.417	8.457	2.167
R-Squared	.071	.068	.092	.080
N	561			

*Statistically significant at .10 percent level (two-tailed test).

Perhaps, the risk of closure must be more immediate, such as a closure in the same county or another plant of the same company in order for statistically significant variations to emerge. On the other hand, even though there was variation in the risk of closure in the 1970s, the absolute rate, 8.0 percent for the entire decade, may not have been significant enough to make unions and workers consider it a critical issue. Inflation or workplace safety and health may have been more pressing issues.

The sizes, signs and statistical significance of the coefficients of the other variables parallel those when employment growth was the key variable. Specifically, collective bargaining coverage and workers are positive and statistically significant when INDEX1, INDEX2 and INDEX4 are the independent variable. RTW is negative and statistically significant in three of the estimates. The findings for 1980 correspond very closely to those reported above.

Third Hypothesis: This hypothesis concerns the use of union bargaining power to obtain contractual protections. Bargaining power entails both union coverage of the industry's workforce (COV) and rivalry among the industry's unions (RIVAL). As indicated in table 5.8 and table 5.9, the extent of bargaining coverage is a positive and significant determinant of the frequency of these provisions in the negotiated agreements. For the 1974 analyses, RIVAL is not a determinant, but becomes positive and statistically significant in three of the equations for 1980.

An alternate version of the union bargaining power hypothesis, particularly as it relates to the differences in the bargaining environment between states that do have right-to-work laws and those that do not, is that two unions, the United Auto Workers (AUTO) and the United Steel Workers (STEEL), possess sufficient strength to obtain their demands irrespective of the bargaining environment. Both unions have organized major plants throughout the United States. Two new dichotomous variables have been specified. The first, AUTO, takes on the value 1 if the contract is negotiated by the United Auto Workers. The second, STEEL, takes on the value 1 if the contract is negotiated by the United Steel Workers. The contracts also are segmented by right-to-work status of the state in which the organized establishment is located and separate analyses are conducted. The results are reported in table 5.13 through table 5.16.

The analyses for 1974 are reported in tables 5.13 and 5.14, with the contracts covering establishments in RTW states analyzed in table 5.13. As expected, the coefficients of AUTO and STEEL are positive and statistically significant in three of the four estimates covering contracts in states where there is no right-to-work law. However, contrary to expectations, these two variables are not significant predictors of contractual outcomes of contracts covering establishments in right-to-work states.

The importance of these two unions in those states without RTW statutes is evident in table 5.14. Both AUTO and STEEL are statistically significant and positive for INDEX1, INDEX2 and INDEX4 in 1974. The impact on the frequency of the provisions also is greater for STEEL than AUTO. There are two somewhat surprising findings reported in table 5.14. First, there is the absence of a statistically significant relationship between GROW74 and variations in the indices. The second one is the lack of explanatory power of both AUTO and STEEL in INDEX3. These provisions simply may not have been bargaining goals for these unions, or they may not have been evaluated to be worth the necessary tradeoff. The analysis was repeated for 1980. The results were very similar to those for 1974. Although not reported here, they are available from the author.

Table 5.13
Determinants of the Incidence of Plant Closure Provisions
Covering Establishments in Right-To-Work States
in Major Collective Bargaining Contracts, 1974
(standard errors in parentheses)

Independent variables	Dependent variable			
	INDEX1	INDEX2	INDEX3	INDEX4
GROW74	-.023	-.200	-.196	-.111*
	(.052)	(.174)	(.134)	(.066)
WORKERS (100s)	.092	.172	-.085	.067
	(.060)	(.201)	(.155)	(.076)
PLANT	.200	-37.709	8.649	-7.164
	(8.260)	(27.641)	(21.247)	(10.471)
MULTI	7.544	-33.764	11.776	-1.724
	(8.494)	(28.424)	(21.850)	(10.768)
AUTO	10.128*	8.641	-2.251	6.661
	(3.459)	(11.575)	(8.898)	(4.385)
STEEL	4.501*	16.166*	-9.919	3.812
	(2.492)	(8.340)	(6.411)	(3.159)
INTERCEPT	-.705	50.396	3.064	13.012
R-Squared	.195	.068	.058	.102
N	104			

*Statistically significant at .10 percent level (two-tailed test).

Table 5.14
Determinants of the Incidence of Plant Closure Provisions
Covering Establishments in States Without Right-To-Work Laws
in Major Collective Bargaining Agreements, 1974
(standard errors in parentheses)

Independent variables	Dependent variable			
	INDEX1	INDEX2	INDEX3	INDEX4
GROW74	-.043	-.055	-.061	-.051
	(.037)	(.087)	(.066)	(.039)
WORKERS (100s)	.035*	.104*	.015	.040*
	(.016)	(.038)	(.029)	(.017)
PLANT	2.110	-3.344	-7.048*	-1.542
	(1.660)	(3.841)	(2.919)	(1.716)
MULTI	10.991*	-7.340	-.009	3.658*
	(1.932)	(4.471)	(3.398)	(1.997)
AUTO	5.304*	17.895*	3.655	8.039*
	(2.403)	(5.560)	(4.226)	(2.484)
STEEL	7.268*	35.140*	-2.087	11.897*
	(1.850)	(4.281)	(3.254)	(1.912)
INTERCEPT	1.611	25.236	15.946	11.101
R-Squared	.151	.156	.026	.124
N	452			

*Statistically significant at .10 percent level (two-tailed test).

Table 5.15
Determinants of the Incidence of Plant Closure Provisions
Covering Establishments in Right-To-Work States
in Major Collective Bargaining Contracts, 1980
(standard errors in parentheses)

Independent variables	Dependent variable			
	INDEX1	INDEX2	INDEX3	INDEX4
GROW80	.223	-.271	-.502*	-.081
	(.137)	(.274)	(.252)	(.131)
RIVAL	.026	.020	.644*	.153
	(.099)	(.198)	(.182)	(.095)
CONC2	4.245	10.585*	-2.852	4.055
	(3.055)	(6.107)	(5.614)	(2.922)
CONC3	-.166	22.090*	-19.120*	.659
	(5.710)	(11.413)	(10.493)	(5.461)
COV2	-1.251	23.085*	23.799*	10.845*
	(4.972)	(9.939)	(9.137)	(4.755)
COV3	-3.713	21.380*	20.658*	8.652*
	(4.473)	(8.941)	(8.219)	(4.278)
WORKERS (100s)	.053	.091	-.128	.017
	(.094)	(.189)	(.173)	(.090)
LENGTH	-.020	.052	-.061	-.012
	(.024)	(.049)	(.045)	(.023)
PLANT	5.137	-28.932	23.762	1.276
	(13.879)	(27.740)	(25.502)	(13.274)
MULTI	11.411	-20.876	26.359	7.076
	(14.255)	(28.490)	(26.191)	(13.633)
INDUS**	----	----	----	----
INTERCEPT	2.953	22.611	-29.944	-.356
R-Squared	.094	.182	.184	.122
N	113			

*Statistically significant at .10 percent level (two-tailed test).

**No industry wide agreements existed in RTW states in the 1980 contract file.

Table 5.16
Determinants of the Incidence of Plant Closure Provisions
Covering Establishments in States Without Right-To-Work Laws
in Major Collective Bargaining Agreements, 1980
(standard errors in parentheses)

Independent variables	Dependent variable			
	INDEX1	INDEX2	INDEX3	INDEX4
GROW80	.051	-.122	-.042	-.015
	(.060)	(.128)	(.089)	(.057)
RIVAL	.027	.219	.483*	.189*
	(.070)	(.149)	(.105)	(.067)
CONC2	-.736	4.675	-4.649*	-2.699*
	(1.710)	(3.651)	(2.561)	(1.650)
CONC3	-.579	11.397*	-3.446	1.697
	(2.844)	(6.075)	(4.261)	(2.746)
COV2	2.635	1.128	-3.405	.748
	(2.038)	(4.352)	(3.053)	(1.967)
COV3	4.429*	11.774*	-3.470	4.290*
	(2.120)	(4.529)	(3.177)	(2.047)
WORKERS (100s)	.068*	.100*	.049	.071*
	(.023)	(.050)	(.035)	(.022)
LENGTH	.000	.146*	-.012	.033
	(.040)	(.087)	(.061)	(.039)
PLANT	3.594	-.595	.863	1.864
	(2.254)	(4.814)	(3.377)	(2.176)
MULTI	9.198*	2.028	4.867	6.323*
	(2.431)	(5.192)	(3.642)	(2.347)
INDUS	7.352*	.204	9.468*	6.094*
	(3.754)	(8.018)	(5.625)	(3.624)
INTERCEPT	.008	13.954	6.574	5.136
R-Squared	.078	.073	.097	.090
N	448			

*Statistically significant at .10 percent level (two-tailed test).

The inability to explain variations in the inclusion of advance notice provisions in these contracts is frustrating. Traditional determinants of bargained outcomes are not effective. But this inability may explain why advance notice of plant closure has been the frontispiece of numerous legislative proposals. The bargaining power of unions may be insufficient to obtain this provision through contract negotiations, and therefore they are seeking this protection through legislations.

Fourth Hypothesis: This hypothesis addresses the differences in bargaining outcomes that may arise in states with right-to-work laws relative to those outcomes in states without right-to-work laws. Although the coefficient of the RTW variable is negative in all equations in table 5.8 and table 5.9, it is statistically significant in only one instance in 1980. The surprising feature is that it is insignificant since the existence of a RTW statute is seen as an indicator that employers have significantly greater political power than unions. Thus, it is expected that this distribution of power would hold in the bargaining relationship, particularly for provisions that may impinge on management rights.

The analyses for 1980 are provided in table 5.15 and table 5.16. The analysis for 1974 is not reported here. The measures of union bargaining power tend to be positive and statistically significant in over half of the estimates covering establishments in right-to-work states. However, there is a lack of consistency in the relative values of COV2 and COV3 in table 5.15. Specifically, COV2 tends to be greater than COV3, whereas the normal expectation is the converse. This may represent a measurement error problem since the estimates of contract coverage are from 1968-1972 and those estimates may no longer be representative of more recent conditions. It also may simply indicate moderately organized industries have pursued these nonwage provisions.

In states without right-to-work laws, the influence of the product market concentration measures is not predictable. However, COV3 and RIVAL emerge as statistically significant determinants in several of the estimates. GROW80 is not a significant determinant in this set of estimates.

Summary

These estimates do not indicate that workers and firms "at risk of closure" have moved toward protections and solutions through the bargained contract. The regression estimates show that contractual outcomes became less sensitive to changes in employment, and instead became more dependent on the bargaining power of the union in 1980 relative to 1974. Even more surprising, however, was the lack of statistical significance of the frequency of closure in the industry as a determinant of successful negotiations over these provisions. Furthermore, the results were not consistent. Variables that were significant in one time period were not in the following one, or vice versa. This lack of robustness raises severe doubts whether the negotiations are sufficiently deterministic.

There are a number of factors which may have contributed to the disappointing findings. First, the cross-sectional analysis of the incidence of provisions may have obscured the changes that did take place. It would have been desirable to track individual contracts from one period to the next, so that the analysis could have been conducted on the actual changes in the contract, but this was not possible. Second, it was not possible to measure other bargaining outcomes that occurred in the same negotiations. Thus, no estimate could be made of the actual tradeoff that may have been required to obtain plant closure provisions.

A troubling feature of the analysis is the very low explanatory power of the equations for variations in INDEX3, the advance notice provisions. The issue of advance notice of plant closure has been one of the most hotly debated topics in the plant closure debate. Is it a question of bargaining goal determination, or of employer resistance to granting this provision? Making this protection the frontispiece of legislative proposals simply may be a response to the inability to obtain it directly in negotiations.

One conclusion that seems quite tenable is that significant bargaining power is required to obtain plant closure contractual protections in RTW states. However, there are restrictions on this conclusion because when two of the most powerful unions were entered explicitly in the specification, AUTO and STEEL, their coefficients generally were not statistically significant. Combining this latter finding with the generally low explanatory power of these equations suggests that we do not have a good understanding of these negotiations and outcomes. Of course, it may simply be the problem mentioned above: union bargaining goals do not necessarily become contract provisions.

NOTES

1. The data set available limits some of the questions that can be asked in this monograph about the presence or absence of these provisions in a contract. Several interesting hypotheses could include the following: first, it is expected that workers in local labor markets where employment alternatives are limited would tend to pursue relocation/transfer right provisions; second, it is expected that relocation/transfer right provisions would be more prevalent where union-management relations have been "good"; and finally, it is expected that bargaining units that are dominated by young and more mobile workers would be more likely to negotiate relocation/transfer right provisions.

2. The "free-rider" problem is when individuals receive the benefit of some collective activity, but do not pay to support the collective activity. For example, the nonpayment of union dues by individuals covered by a collective bargaining contract is a free-rider problem.

3. The frequencies in both 1974 and 1980 of the plant closure provisions are as follows:

PROVISION	1974 percent	1980 percent
SUB	22	26
SEVRANCE	39	38
RELOCATE	8	11
TRANPLT	15	19
TRANHIRE	5	7
TRANCOMB	7	3
SHUTDWN	14	15
CHANGE	10	11
Number of Contracts	631	676

4. To ensure comparability, the set of states having right-to-work laws in 1974 were used throughout the analysis. New Hampshire was not included because it does not have a specific right-to-work statute.

5. This assumes that these provisions represent primarily union imposed constraints on management rights. This seems like a reasonable assumption for most of these provisions.

6. See Audrey Freedman (1978). She wrote: "Still it seems axiomatic that as an individual job hunter's chances in the open labor market worsen, job security becomes more important." (p. 67)

7. Newman (1983) has demonstrated that the favorable economic growth consequences of right-to-work laws are not purely a Southern phenomenon.

8. There is a simultaneity question with the structure of bargaining relationship variables. Specifically, Hendricks and Kahn (1982) determined that the actual structure used is a function of industry and union characteristics.

9. Although the demarcation is necessitated by the data sets, it also is fortuitous given that Lilien (1982) has suggested that the structural shift accelerated after 1973.

10. Three-digit closure rates are available on request from the author.

11. The 3-digit concentration ratio was calculated as follows:

$$CONC_j = \sum_{i=1}^{n} \left(CON_{ij} \right) \left(\frac{VS_{ij}}{VS_j} \right)$$

where

$CONC_j$ = concentration ratio in the jth 3-digit industry.

CON_{ij} = percent of shipments accounted for by the 4 largest firms in in the ith 4-digit industry of the jth 3-digit industry.

VS_{ij} = Value of shipments of all firms in the ith 4-digit industry of the jth 3-digit industry.

VS_j = Value of shipments of all firms in the jth 3-digit industry.

12. Cappelli (1983) used two other measures to address a related concept, variations in the demand for union labor. He used the trend in import penetration in the particular industry and the trend in union coverage in the particular industry. The trend in union coverage is a more direct measure of the pressure on the union sector to attempt to stabilize employment demand. For example, employment growth could be stable, but the unionized sector could be declining in number and the non-unionized sector could be increasing in number. Since the emphasis is on overall change, however, employment growth will continue to be used.

13. Using equal weights implies that each provision is equally desirable or effective. This is a tenuous assumption, particularly when only eight provisions are involved and may be partially responsible for the results that follow.

14. A series of regressions were run incorporating whether the bargained agreement included a management rights clause. The coefficient on this variable was not statistically significant.

Chapter 6   Synthesis and Conclusions

The principal economic impact of plant closure on workers is the earnings loss that they may experience. First, there is the direct earnings loss due job loss. Second, there is the initial reduction in wages because the available opportunities simply do not pay as much as the former job. Third, the earnings profile of the worker may be reduced because his/her career has been disrupted. Another type of loss is the deferred compensation the firm may owe its workers, but which is never paid because the plant closes.

The deferred compensation arises from compensation schedules that pay junior workers less than the value of their marginal product and pay senior workers more than the value of their marginal product. There is nothing inherently wrong with such a schedule. However, if some event occurs that interferes with the worker being employed until the deferred compensation has been paid back, this unpaid deferred compensation may establish an obligation from the firm to its workers beyond the closure. This may represent a classic case of social costs since the firm's action imposes costs on people not party to the decision. The question is: Can collective bargaining play a role in minimizing social costs while promoting greater productive capacity?

Collective bargaining and plant closure are linked in three ways. First, judicial interpretations of the National Labor

Relations Act (NLRA) have held that the employer must negotiate with the union over the effects of closing a plant, the closing bargain. Second, the current judicial interpretation is that there is no duty to bargain over the decision to close one plant of a multiplant operation. There are, however, certain ambiguities in this interpretation that limit its applicability. Third, a union and an employer may use the formal bargaining process to negotiate contract provisions covering plant closure.

To understand and evaluate the role that collective bargaining could play, both the case law that has evolved in the formulation of the judicial interpretations and the actual contract provisions negotiated in major collective bargaining agreements have been examined. Coincident with the analysis of the case law, several rules and procedures, which have been suggested to expedite the determination of whether there is a duty to bargain over the decision, also have been studied.

The examination of the judicial interpretation of the duty to bargain found several troublesome areas. First, substantive labor law has been formulated in the plant closure area based on cases in which the parties to the dispute had not negotiated a formal contract. The closure occurred almost on the heels of the union winning the representation election. Thus, a determination has been made on the efficacy of collective bargaining resolving an issue even though the parties have never bargained. As pointed out in the text, the most recent U.S. Supreme Court ruling on this issue occurred in *First National Maintenance Corporation v. National Labor Relations Board,* a case in which the parties did not have an established bargaining relationship.

Second, there has been an overriding concern with the terminology used in cases of displacement rather than with the outcome. For example, subcontracting has been differentiated from replacing existing employees with independent contractors. The outcome has been the same, the process very similar, but the duty to bargain over the decision differs. A similar demarcation is occurring between plant closure and relocation. In both instances a facility is closed, and the reason for closure may be quite similar—the firm is no longer competitive at the location—but the case law treats these quite differently.

The case law draws the marked distinction between the rights and privileges of the owners of physical capital as opposed to the rights and privileges of the owners of human capital. Human capital is not positioned equally with physical capital in its ability to respond to economic change. However, giving priority to the owners of human capital in all situations would move us to a system of property rights in jobs, which is not necessarily desirable. As was stated in *Adams Dairy,* "union membership is not a guarantee against legitimate or justifiable discharge or discharge motivated by economic necessity." What is necessary is a balancing between the rights of the owners of physical capital and human capital. Collective bargaining may be uniquely positioned to conduct this balancing test.

The major concerns over the use of collective bargaining to mitigate the plant closure problem are establishing criteria which (a) require bargaining only in those instances in which the circumstances suggest a positive probability of success, and (b) introduce certainty into the process as to who must bargain and what shall constitute good faith bargaining. Perhaps, however, there has been more concern than warranted about not requiring bargaining in low probability cases. Recall that there were 619 plant closings in 1982, a year in which the economy was mired in a recession. The relatively infrequent nature of plant closing increases the attractiveness of collective bargaining as a policy alternative.

Formal collective bargaining already occurs over plant closure, or at least, over provisions to minimize the effects of closure. Contractual provisions that have been negotiated include severance pay, supplemental unemployment benefits, relocation allowances, transfer or preferential hiring rights, and advance notice in case of shutdown or major technological change. The concern from the policy perspective is whether management and labor have used formal contract negotiations to obtain protections and to develop solutions for workers and firms "at risk of closure."

The results of the econometric analysis of major collective bargaining agreements (631 contracts in 1974 and 676 contracts in 1980) did not find that workers at risk were obtaining these protections. Variation in closure rates by industry was not a significant determinant of variations in contractual outcomes. Instead, the regression estimates showed that the contractual outcomes became less sensitive to changes in employment, and instead became more dependent on the bargaining power of the union in 1980 relative to 1974. The results also were not consistent. This lack of robustness (a) pointed out the difficulty of modeling some processes and outcomes, and (b) raised doubts about whether formal negotiations could be relied on to accommodate these disruptions.

Therefore, amending the National Labor Relations Act's definition of mandatory topics of bargaining under "terms and other conditions of employment" to include bargaining over the decision to close may be one policy alternative for the plant closure dilemma. There are positive and negative aspects of this approach. The most obvious negative aspect is that the NLRA covers only those plants and workplaces where employees have elected a bargaining agent. Since plant closures are not restricted to unionized plants, protection will not be afforded in all instances. However, workers in nonunionized facilities generally are not protected by the provisions of the National Labor Relations Act. Although this lack of coverage is problematic, it is not fatal.

A positive feature of using the NLRA is that coverage is uniform throughout the United States. As mentioned earlier, two states have statutes placing obligations on employers in the event of closure, legislation has been proposed in many other states, and the National Employment Priorities Act (H.R. 2847) has been introduced in the U.S. Congress. However, state-by-state adoption of legislation would only increase the competition among the states. Kochan (1979) wrote:

> those states most interested in stemming the tide of
> plant closings and job loss are most likely to act,
> but by doing so, may further increase the incentives
> of businesses to locate in the southern states that do
> not pass this type of legislation (p. 19).

Unions may find fault with this approach because they will be expected to use up their bargaining capital in order to obtain the protections that they would prefer be provided through legislation. The greater the number of areas prescribed by governmental regulation, the more bargaining power can be concentrated in other areas. Management also may disagree with the proposal because it places a greater burden on them than currently required. Given the unique circumstance of each workplace and the preferences of workers, collective bargaining may be ideally suited to developing solutions to this problem. Regulation and bargaining are both designed to get employers and unions to do something they do not want to do and, therefore, to a degree they are substitute policies.

What is being considered is a policy that neither management nor labor prefers. But perhaps that is the only type of policy possible. "The political problem is to shift the focus of public discussion away from the fruitless search for painless solutions to the question of how costs of adjustment can be allocated in the most equitable way." (Martin 1983, p. 105)

The proposal of this monograph attempts to permit bargaining to minimize the earnings loss of workers while exploring more profitable opportunities for the firm. The proposal is based on Coase's (1971) concept of minimizing social cost while maximizing the value of production. As always, the difficulty is making an abstract concept operational. The following *per se* rule and implementation procedures are proposed.

1. Firms are required to notify the NLRB and the union of the plan to close one part of an operation or to relocate. This notice should contain a detailed explanation of the reasons for closure and financial data as appropriate.

2. The NLRB quickly determines whether bargaining might be fruitful using the criteria established in *Brooks-Scanlon:* whether the reasons for closure are beyond the control of the parties to the collective bargaining agreement.

3. Information bargaining occurs in those instances where it is determined that bargaining might be fruitful.

4. Based on the information provided, the NLRB, the union or bargaining unit, and the firm determine whether further bargaining is appropriate.

5. Bargaining continues in those instances where two of the three (the NLRB, the union or bargaining unit, and the firm) think progress is being made and/or a solution is possible, but for no more than 90 days after the initial notice.

6. If bargaining has been in good faith, but no agreement is reached within the time period, the firm is free to proceed with its action.

7. The firm is required to bargain over the effects.

This proposal has the basic premise that management and labor will want to obtain a bargain that leads to profitable operations and is the best alternative in the labor market. If the concessions necessary to maintain profitable operations require wage cuts greater than necessary as dictated by market alternatives, no agreement will or should be reached. If operations as profitable as the alternative can be achieved, management will and should stay at the existing plant. If no agreement is possible within the parameters, effects bargaining can be used to obtain the deferred compensation.

Wachter and Wascher's (1983) examination of the displaced worker problem led them to conclude that the earnings losses experienced by displaced workers can be avoided only by avoiding job loss in the first place. Job specific skills, seniority pay and union differentials all result in wages above the alternatives available in the market. Job training, special assistance programs or employment vouchers are unlikely to generate employment opportunities at previous wage levels. Since public controls, such as direct employment protection, impose significant costs on the overall economy, Wachter and Wascher suggest collective bargaining initiatives trading wage premiums for enhanced job security.

The proposal of this monograph is in the same spirit as their conclusion. Neither management nor labor have perfect foresight. Formal negotiations every two or three years cannot accommodate all contingencies. Equity considerations suggest that workers be afforded the opportunity to minimize earnings and/or job loss. Recognizing that doing so also imposes costs on employers, the proposal has been structured to be flexible and to expedite the bargaining process.

Requiring decision bargaining is only one element, but a major one, of a comprehensive policy toward the plant closure problem. Bargaining will not result in preserving jobs in all instances. Other programs need to be in place to assist workers when closure is the only alternative. But in devising programs, consideration must be given to the "managerial, institutional and political factors that determine the effectiveness of policies in practice." (Bacow 1980, p. 132) Expansive legislative proposals that prescribe the behavior of firms intending to close are not consistent with the managerial, institutional and political constructs of our economic system. Instead, states have started to turn away from the regulatory initiatives and have been developing assistance programs for displaced workers, such as job clubs, job fairs and retraining programs.

It is important not to stop just with assistance programs for displaced workers. There are other institutions in place which, with minor changes, could become flexible enough to smooth the adjustment to economic change. One is the tax deductibility of training costs associated with developing a new skill. Given the adjustment problems of human capital in the presence of economic change, it is incongruous that investments to deepen one's human capital in an obsolete skill are deductible for federal income tax purposes whereas investments to broaden one's human capital and develop new skills are not deductible. Another change would be permitting workers to obtain training while receiving unemployment compensation. (It should be noted that this is permitted in some states under certain circumstances.) Since the unemployment insurance system is funded by employer contributions, it would seem appropriate that these funds be used to support retraining efforts necessitated by industrial change.

The final point is that funds be available to study the viability of Employee Stock Ownership Plans (ESOPs) when closure is being considered. Wintner's (1983) results have demonstrated that ESOPs can be viable in some instances. (In fact, her results are very supportive of the potential for collective bargaining in addressing the plant closure problem.) Since workers generally are subjecting themselves to double jeopardy in ESOPs—a possible wage reduction plus placing their savings at risk—the viability of the ESOP should be studied thoroughly.

In conclusion, as we consider the plant closure issue and the problem of displaced workers, one criterion should be kept in mind as alternative policies are considered. Any program contemplated should not increase the firm's direct cost of using labor relative to capital. Increasing the cost of labor will simply make the adoption of new technology more attractive for employers, possibly exacerbating the problem.

Appendix

Displaced Older Workers

The problems displacement causes for older workers require special mention. Hall (1982) has shown that firms in the United States provide near-lifetime employment (more than 20 years) for a significant part of the labor force. For example, 51.1 percent of all men are likely to work 20 years or more for the same firm. A recent Department of Labor (1983) study shows that many workers already have been employed with the same firm for a relatively long time. For workers between the ages of 40 and 44 years, 42.7 percent have worked for the same firm for more than 10 years and for those between the ages of 50 to 54 years, 56.5 percent have worked for the same firm for more than 10 years. If it is assumed that the revealed behavior reflects the expectations of workers, the loss of their job can be a severe blow.

Perhaps more problematic is that many incentives cause the impact of closure on older workers to be very severe in the short run. The usual process of attrition and gradual reduction in employment prior to closure returns younger workers (less senior) to the labor market first. That attrition permits these younger workers to search for available openings when fewer workers are competing for them.

When closure finally occurs, the older workers are returned to the labor market simultaneously. This fact is exacerbated by policies which require workers to stay until closure in order to receive severance pay and other related benefits. Their work skills may be somewhat obsolete, their job search skills have atrophied and their numbers may greatly exceed the available openings in the market when they begin to seek new employment. Moreover, since their skills tend to be firm- or industry-specific, they may have significant difficulty in transferring them to other employment opportunities.

Several studies have documented the extent of the wage loss incurred by workers who have been displaced by plant closure. These are instructive even though it is argued in the monograph that the initial loss can be an artifact of the firm's compensation schedule. Arlene Holen et al. (1981) developed estimates of earnings losses from a sample of 9,500 workers who were impacted by 42 different plant closings in 21 different states from 1968 to 1972. The analysis was restricted to nine different industries.

The differences in earnings loss by age group are very striking. Workers under the age of 40 experienced a 13.4 percent drop in average earnings in the year after closure relative to the year before closure. Workers over the age of 40 experienced a 39.9 percent reduction in earnings in the year after closure. Furthermore, the average earnings of workers over 40 in the year after closure were *less* than the average earnings of those under 40, as indicated in table A.1. In addition, the labor force activity of the older group declined by approximately 33 percentage points, whereas the reduction in labor force activity for the younger workers was approximately 7 percentage points.

A study of a plant closure in Western Michigan further demonstrates the impact on older workers (McAlinden 1981). The average seniority for the workers left at the time of the closing was over 17 years. The average age of the workers was approximately 45 years. The wages for skilled, semi-skilled and unskilled workers had been $10.22, $9.97 and $9.43 per hour, respectively. Approximately 11 months after the closing, the workers were surveyed, and the average hourly wages for those who had found jobs were $10.02, $7.51 and $6.52 for skilled, semi-skilled and unskilled workers, respectively. Skilled workers suffered only a 2 percent loss in wages, but semi-skilled and unskilled workers' losses were 25 percent and 31 percent, respectively. Furthermore, over one-half of the workers were still unemployed at the time of the survey, with the largest proportion of them being semi-skilled and unskilled.

Table A.1
Mean Real Earnings and Labor Force Activity of Males
by Age, Before and After Closure*

	Under 40		Over 40	
	Year prior to closing	Year after closing	Year prior to closing	Year after closing
Average earnings	$5,705	$4,943	$8,111	$4,877
Percent change		-13.4%		-39.9%
Full-time labor force activity (%)	82.9	76.1	93.5	60.1

SOURCE: Calculations based on data provided in Arlene Holen et al., *Earnings Losses of Workers Displaced by Plant Closings,* Public Research Institute of the Center for Naval Analysis, CRC 423, December 1981.
*1970 Constant dollars.

Older workers suffer significant short term losses because there are just fewer job offers available for them. Older workers may be more expensive to hire than younger workers because defined benefit pension plans are most costly to provide for older workers than for younger workers (Barnow and Ehrenberg 1979). Assuming a 6 percent rate of return, $1 of pension benefits will cost an employer $1 for a worker retiring in a year, whereas the cost will be $.17 for the 35-year-old worker who won't retire for 30 years. As a result, even though an older worker and a younger worker may be willing to work for the same wage, the former will be more costly to hire if pension benefits are part of the compensation. It has been estimated that approximately 70 percent of private pension plans are defined benefit plans.

Older workers may restrict their job search to the local market because they are homeowners, and to that subset of relatively high paying jobs because of their wage expectations. Thus, their expected duration of unemployment tends to be longer and their expected wage loss is likely to be greater.

Holen's estimates were of the earnings losses individuals incurred within five years of closure. Jacobson and Thomason (1979) estimated lifetime earnings losses. Their analysis determined that the lifetime earnings loss associated with displacement tends to increase as the unemployment rate in the local labor market increases. Second, the earnings loss tends to be inversely related to the size of the local labor market.

REFERENCES

Abowd, John M. and Orley Ashenfelter. "Anticipated Unemployment, Temporary Layoffs, and Compensating Wage Differentials," in Sherwin Rosen, ed., *Studies in Labor Markets* (Chicago: University of Chicago Press, 1981).

Abraham, Katherine G. and James L. Medoff. "Length of Service, Terminations and the Nature of the Employment Relationship," Working Paper No. 1086, Cambridge, MA: National Bureau of Economic Research, March 1983.

Bacow, Laurence. *Bargaining for Job Safety and Health* (Cambridge, MA: MIT Press, 1980).

Baily, Martin Neil. "Wages and Employment Under Uncertain Demand." *Review of Economic Studies* 41 (1974) pp. 37-50.

Baily, Martin Neil. "On the Theory of Layoffs and Unemployment." *Econometrica* 45 (July 1977) pp. 1043-1063.

Barnow, Burt S. and Ronald G. Ehrenberg. "The Costs of Defined Pension Plans and Firm Adjustments." *Quarterly Journal of Economics* 93 (November 1979) pp. 523-540.

Birch, David. *The Job Generation Process* (Cambridge, MA: MIT Program on Neighborhood and Regional Change, 1979).

Bluestone, Barry and Bennett Harrison. *Capital and Communities: The Causes and Consequences of Private Disinvestment* (Washington, DC: The Progressive Alliance, 1980).

Bluestone, Barry and Bennett Harrison. *The Deindustrialization of America* (New York: Basic Books, Inc., 1982).

Bosanac, Paul. "Concession Bargaining, Work Transfers, and Mid-contract Modification: Los Angeles Marine Hardware Company." *Labor Law Journal* (February 1983) pp. 72-70.

Bureau of National Affairs, Inc. *Layoffs, Plant Closings and Concession Bargaining, Summary Report for 1982.* Washington, DC, 1983.

Calabresi, Guido. *The Costs of Accidents: A Legal and Economic Analysis* (New Haven, CT: Yale University Press, 1970).

Cappelli, Peter. "Concession Bargaining and the National Economy." *Proceedings,* Thirty-Fifth Annual Meeting, Industrial Relations Research Association, Madison, WI: IRRA, 1983, pp. 362-372.

Coase, Ronald. "The Problem of Social Cost," in William Breit and Harold M. Hockman, eds., *Readings in Microeconomics* (New York: Holt, Rinehart & Winston, 1971).

"Duty to Bargain About Termination of Operations: *Brockway Motor Trucks v. NLRB." Harvard Law Review* 92 (January 1979) pp. 768-780.

Ehrenberg, Ronald G., Leif Danziger and Gee San. "Cost of Living Clauses in Union Contracts," Working Paper No. 998, Cambridge, MA: National Bureau of Economic Research, October 1982.

Farber, Henry S. "Bargaining Theory, Wage Outcomes, and the Occurrence of Strikes: An Econometric Analysis." *The American Economic Review* 68 (June 1978) pp. 262-271.

Freedman, Audrey. *Security Bargains Reconsidered: SUB, Severance Pay, Guaranteed Work* (New York: The Conference Board, 1978).

Freeman, Richard B. and James L. Medoff. "New Estimates of Private Sector Unionism in the United States." *Industrial and Labor Relations Review* 32 (January 1979) pp. 143-174.

Gerhart, Paul F. "Determinants of Bargaining Outcomes in Local Government Labor Negotiations." *The Industrial and Labor Relations Review* 29 (April 1976) pp. 331-351.

Gordus, Jeanne Prial, Paul Jarley and Louis A. Ferman. *Plant Closings and Economic Dislocation* (Kalamazoo, MI: The W.E. Upjohn Institute for Employment Research, 1981).

Hall, Robert E. "The Importance of Lifetime Jobs in the U.S. Economy." *The American Economic Review* 72 (September 1982) pp. 716-724.

Heinsz, Timothy J. "The Partial-Closing Conundrum: The Duty to Bargain in Good Faith." *Duke Law Journal* (February 1981) pp. 77-113.

Hendricks, Wallace. "Labor Market Structure and Union Wage Levels." *Economic Inquiry* 13 (September 1975) pp. 401-416.

Hendricks, Wallace E. and Lawrence M. Kahn. "The Determinants of Bargaining Structure in U.S. Manufacturing Industries." *Industrial and Labor Relations Review* 35 (January 1982) pp. 181-195.

Hendricks, Wallace E. and Lawrence M. Kahn. "Cost-of-Living Clauses in Union Contracts: Determinants and Effects." *Industrial Labor Relations Review* 36 (April 1983) pp. 447-460.

Holen, Arlene, Christopher Jehn and Robert P. Trost. *Earnings Losses of Workers Displaced by Plant Closings* (Alexandria, VA: The Center for Naval Analyses, Public Research Institute, CRC 423, December 1981).

Jacobson, Louis and Janet Thomason. *Earnings Loss Due to Displacement.* (Alexandria, VA: The Center for Naval Analyses, Public Research Institute, August 1979).

Kasl, Stanislav V. and Sidney Cobb. "Some Mental Health Consequences of Plant Closings and Job Loss," in Louis A. Ferman and Jeanne P. Gordus, eds., *Mental Health and the Economy* (Kalamazoo, MI: The W. E. Upjohn Institute for Employment Research, 1979).

Kassalow, Everett M. "Concession Bargaining - Something Old, But Also Something Quite New." *Proceedings* Thirty-Fifth Annual Meeting, Industrial Relations Research Association, Madison, WI: IRRA, 1983, pp. 372-382.

Killingsworth, Charles C. "Collective Bargaining Approaches to Employee Displacement Problems (Outside the Railroad Industry)," in *Studies Relating to Collective Bargaining Agreements and Practices Outside the Railroad Industry,* Appendix Volume IV to the Report of the Presidential Railroad Commission (Washington, DC: U.S. Government Printing Office, February 1962).

Klaper, Martin J. "The Right to Relocate Work During the Term of an Existing Collective Bargaining Agreement." *Labor Law Journal* (February 1983) pp. 94-103.

Kochan, Thomas A. "The Federal Role in Economic Dislocations: Toward a Better Mix of Public and Private Efforts," prepared for the Office of the Assistant Secretary for Policy, Evaluation and Research, U.S. Department of Labor, October 1979.

Kochan, Thomas A. and Richard N. Block. "An Interindustry Analysis of Bargaining Outcomes: Preliminary Evidence From Two-Digit Industries." *Quarterly Journal of Economics* 91 (August 1977) pp. 431-452.

Lazear, Edward P. "Agency, Earnings Profiles, Productivity, and Hours Restrictions." *American Economic Review* 71 (September 1981) pp. 606-620.

Lazear, Edward P. "Severance Pay, Pensions, and Efficient Mobility," Working Paper No. 854 (Cambridge, MA: National Bureau of Economic Research, February 1982).

Levinson, Harold M. "Unionism, Concentration and Wage Changes: Toward a Unified Theory." *The Industrial and Labor Relations Review* 20 (January 1967) pp. 198-205.

Lilien, David M. "Sectoral Shifts and Cyclical Unemployment." *Journal of Political Economy* 90 (August 1982) pp. 777-793.

Martin, Philip L. *Labor Displacement and Public Policy* (Lexington, MA: Lexington Books, 1983).

McAlinden, S. *The Closing at AP Parts* (Preliminary Report) 1981.

McKenzie, Richard B. *Restrictions on Business Mobility* (Washington, DC: American Enterprise Institute for Public Policy Research, 1979).

McKenzie, Richard B. "The Case for Plant Closures." *Policy Review* 15 (Winter 1981) pp. 119-133.

McKenzie, Richard B. and Bruce Yandle. "State Plant Closing Laws: Their Union Support." *Journal of Labor Research* 3 (Winter 1982) pp. 101-110.

Miscimarra, Philip A. *The NLRB and Managerial Discretion: Plant Closings, Relocations, Subcontracting and Automation* (Philadelphia, PA: University of Pennsylvania, Industrial Research Unit, 1983).

Mitchell, Daniel J.B. "Is Union Wage Determination at a Turning Point?" *Proceedings,* Thirty-Fifth Annual Meeting, Industrial Relations Research Association, Madison, WI: IRRA, 1983, pp. 354-361.

National Labor Relations Board. *Forty-Fifth Annual Report of the National Labor Relations Board* (Washington, DC: U.S. Government Printing Office, 1981).

Nelson, Richard B. "State Labor Legislation Enacted in 1982." *Monthly Labor Review* 106 (January 1983) pp. 44-63.

Nelson, Richard B. "State Labor Legislation Enacted in 1983." *Monthly Labor Review* 107 (January 1984) pp. 59-75.

Newman, Robert J. "Industry Migration and Growth in the South." *The Review of Economics and Statistics* 65 (February 1983) pp. 76-86.

Prosten, Richard. "The Longest Season: Union Organizing in the Last Decade," a/k/a "How Come One Team Has to Play With Its Shoelaces Tied Together?" *Proceedings,* Thirty-First Annual Meeting, Industrial Relations Research Association, Madison, WI: IRRA, 1979.

Rabin, Robert J. "*Fibreboard* and the Termination of Bargaining Unit Work: The Search for Standards in Defining the Scope of the Duty to Bargain." *Columbia Law Review* 71 (1971) pp. 803-806.

Reich, Robert B. "Regulation by Confrontation or Negotiation?" *Harvard Business Review* 59 (May-June 1981) pp. 82-93.

Sayles, Leonard, R. and George Strauss. "Conflicts With the Local Union." *Harvard Business Review* 30 (November-December 1952) pp. 84-92.

Schmenner, Roger W. *Making Business Location Decisions* (Englewood Cliffs, NJ: Prentice-Hall, 1982).

Schmenner, Roger W. "Every Factory Has a Life Cycle." *Harvard Business Review* 61 (March-April 1983) pp. 121-129.

Schwarz, Thomas J. "Plant Relocation or Partial Termination - The Duty to Decision Bargain." *Fordham Law Review* 39 (1970) pp. 81-102.

Shultz, George P. and Arnold R. Weber. *Strategies for the Displaced Worker* (New York: Harper & Row, 1966).

St. Antoine, Theodore J. "The Role of Law," in Jack Steiber, Robert B. McKersie and D. Quinn Mills, eds., *U.S. Industrial Relations 1950-1980: A Critical Assessment* (Madison, WI: Industrial Relations Research Association, 1981).

Stern, Robert N., K. Haydn Wood and Tove Helland Hammer. *Employee Ownership in Plant Shutdowns: Prospects for Employment Stability* (Kalamazoo, MI: The W. E. Upjohn Institute for Employment Research, 1979).

Stoikov, Vladimir. "The Allocation of the Cost of Displaced Labor and Severance Pay." *Journal of Human Resources* 4 (Spring 1969) pp. 192-204.

Swift, Robert A. *The NLRB and Management Decision Making* (Philadelphia, PA: University of Pennsylvania, Industrial Research Unit, 1974).

U.S. Congress. Congressional Budget Office. *Dislocated Workers: Issues and Federal Options* (Washington, DC: U.S. Government Printing Office, 1982).

U.S. Department of Commerce. Bureau of the Census. *Census of Manufactures, 1972, 1977* (Washington, DC: Government Printing Office, 1975 and 1980).

U.S. Department of Labor. *Characteristics of Major Collective Bargaining Agreements* (1980 - Magnetic Tape, 1974 - Cards).

U.S. Department of Labor. Bureau of Labor Statistics. *Employment and Earnings, 1909-1978 and Supplement* (Washington, DC: U.S. Government Printing Office, 1978 and 1982).

U.S. Department of Labor. Bureau of Labor Statistics. *Job Tenure and Occupational Change, 1981,* Bulletin 2162, January 1983.

Wachter, Michael and William L. Wascher. *Labor Market Policies in Response to Structural Changes in Labor Demand.* Paper presented at Symposium on Industrial Change and Public Policy, Federal Reserve Bank of Kansas City, August 1983.

Weber, Arnold R. and David P. Taylor. "Procedures for Employee Displacement: Advance Notice of Plant Shutdown." *Journal of Business* 36 (July 1963) pp. 302-315.

Weiss, Leonard. "Concentration and Labor Earnings." *The American Economic Review* 56 (March 1966) pp. 96-117.

Werner, Jack, Wayne Wendling and Norbert Budde. "A Comparison of Probit, Logit, Discriminant and OLS: The Physician's Location Choice Problem." *Proceedings,* Business and Economics Statistics Section. Washington, DC: American Statistical Association, 1979.

Wintner, Linda. *Employee Buyouts: An Alternative to Plant Closings,* Research Bulletin No. 140 (New York: The Conference Board, 1983).